Senseless Murder

Senseless Murder

by
Keno Mapp

Kenosworld

Copyright © 2001 Revised Copyright © 2005
by
Keno Mapp
All rights reserved.
No part of this book may be reproduced or transmitted
in any form or by means, electronic or mechanical, including
photocopying, recording, or by any information storage and
retrieval system, without the written permission of the Publisher,
except where permitted by law.
For information address:
www.kenosworld.com
First Printing. Printed on Acid-free paper and produced and bound in
the United States of America.
Place of publication Oakland, California
Photos by Jim Dennise, Dano Perez, Tracy Bartlow, Cina Wakasa,
Jayson Valencia & Keno Mapp
Cover Design by Keno Mapp and Cina Wakasa aka Anna
ISBN:0-9768518-0-6
Library of Congress Control Number: 2005903879

Give Thanks,

To those around that have helped me smile, me cry, me love, me fly. My mother and Aunts, nine in all for showing me how to be a gentelman. My grandmother and Great grandmother for their strength and wisdom. My brother (Billy) and little sister (Princess) for surviving the lifes days. My father for his knowledge in the lifegame.
The sun, moon, stars, air, life, love, tears, dreams and the earth.
My friends, Reha, Tony Gits, Jay Asman, Sudden Sam, Dano Perez, Philip & Lisa Bautista, Marcus Aguilar, Ira Black, Angelo Moore, Dr. Madd Vibe & Fishbone, Maggie, Mike Dolly, Beata Schafer, Jayson Valencia, Jeanette Brandt and Family, Brentwood Film Festival, Bruce@awesometux, Antonio Williams, Dwayne Wiggins, Lina Elawar, Hanno Brunn, Steven Lawrance & Effie, Juan Richardson, Durga McBroom, Doug Polhamius, Cina Wakasa (Anna) for all the stars, Kevin Carnes, Atma Anur, Richardo Scales and Baysound Records, Joanna, Pastor Amos Brown, Carol Ogilvy, Rene Otterman, Didi, Wolfgang, Stefon, Sonja Haluzan, Mie, Tara Keckeisen, BT Publishing, B.W. Winfield, Sasha, Gabbie Traitz and the Soulmachine, Cecilia Murillo, Barbara Kirton, Amo, Micheal Govan I & II, James Polk and The Polk Family, Jessica Holter & The Punany Poets (Jus Bea, Kween, DJ, Lucky 7, Myron, Mis Little, Femi, Michelle Blunt & Yolanda Washington), Rochelle Buford, Jim and Donna Halow, Trinity Capital, 3rd Baptish Church S.F., The Legendary Christopher Washington, Intersection for the Arts, Jannis and the NN Train Berlin, Jim Dennis, Katja, Rose Benkiser, Ya Shen, Ying Ji Huang, Yuan Zhu, my son Keno2 and daugther, Ashley, God and those that helped me to see that my words did help.

ACKNOWLEDGEMENTS

We all go through it.
Sometimes, the sun shines hot and other times, the rain just pours.
It's easy to lose yourself on this planet and if we are unable to embrace the truth of ourselves, we will never be able to fly.

Bestdays,
Keno

Table of Contents

1   Dreams

Crazy Dreams	2
Sandman	3
Dreams	4
View of Love	5
I had a dream	6
A Gift	7
Beat'em Join'em	8
Run and Hide	9
All will be	10
Out there	11

2   Life

Beauty within Beast	13
In touch	14
Blown	15
Directions	16
Mommy	17
Sweet Dreams	19
Tick Toc	20
Bgood	21
Letter To Life	22
Real All The Time	23
Enough	24
Here is a Place	26
Auntie	27
America	28
No words	29
No answers	30

3 Heart

Keep the faith	33
Will Not Falter	35
Go on	36
New Born	37
Space	39
Passing Judgment	40
Good vs. Bad	42
Art surrounds	43
Winter is Coming	44
A day Without	45
So Maybe It's Not Me	47
Mine Mouth	48
No Dream	49
The Gardener	50
I am clear	51
One's Imagination	52
More Words	53
I Shall Sing	54
Sticks and Stones	55
Easy	56

4 Fly

Angels	58
Sunbeams	59
Be proud	60
Fly'in	61
No Journal	62
The Buffalo	63
In God We Trust	64
Prosperity	65
Poetry End	66

So Much Life	67
Stuck in place	68
Mother's mother's mother	69
Nothing...	71
Did u no	72
See Ya	73
Soulmate	74
Still your flower	76
Left Handed	77

5   *Love*

Just Words	79
Viva Amour	80
Lovemenot	81
How and Why	82
Love and Aloha	83
Love them	84
Love, love more	85
Flower bed	87
4those that love	88
Only Dreams	90
Eggs in the snow	91
Music is	92
So hard	93
Food and Water	94
Mistakes	95

6   *Butterfly*

Thanks for u	98
Fallen Angels	99
Next Time	101
Lost and Found	103

Ripe Fruit	104
Kiss me	106
Smile	107
Had a Wife	108
Tender maps	109
Desert Flower	110
Another Step	111
Much More	112
Well, who?	113
Love is like trees	114

7 Bullet

Innocent children	116
My Prison	117
No	118
Some Lie	119
Monsters	120
No Dicks	121
Love, right?	122
Who's True	124
Cars	125
My Skin	126
Mercy	127
No smell	128
Here I am	129
No excuse	130
Agony	131

8 Stars

Sun Break	133
There's life	134
Our Mother's Child	135

A star	137
Oneself	138
Her baby	139
Water	140
Start today	142
Wonderful day	143
Hold On	145
Us	146
Child's Giggle	147
I am me	148
Getting Hard	149
The Instrument	150
Adam	151
Me	152
Don't Cry	153
Sleepy	154
Mother's Arms	155
Mother told me	156
Close Your Eyes	158

9 Lovers

So What	160
Romeo & Juliet	161
Hold my Hand	163
Can't	164
Loves	165
The lucky Ones	166
Keep Us Warm	168
Lastnight	169
Beata	170
By My Own Hand	172
Roses are Red	173
What I would do	174
I wish you Love	176

Talk to me	177
Careless	178
I love her	179
Could it be U	181
Just left	182
Missed you	183
Be still	184
Spank Me	185

10   *Sex*

For I miss	187
Bad Thing	188
Mak'in Love	189
Sweet Sexy	190
Sharing	191
Say babe	192
Faith Alone	194
Give Thanks	196
Dinner	197
Morning	198

11   *Tears*

Own Tears	200
Love your Heart	201
Faith	202
Promises	203
It's over	204
Don't give up	206
The Dark	207
Matters not	208
Hearing Heals	209
Just Falling	210

Love lost	*212*
Never Over	*213*
Most Don't Care	*215*
Where do we go	*216*
Got to fly	*217*
Sometimes	*218*

12 *Planet*

Who Are You	*220*
Dirty Streets	*221*
Harvest	*223*
Home	*224*
More	*225*
Funny	*226*
Is it so	*227*
Be Counted	*228*
Our air	*229*
Ever so clear	*230*
I Can	*232*
Closed doors	*233*
Planet Round	*234*
Senseless Murder	*236*

You need you...

Dreams

Dreams
 `dreamer, dreaming,
day-dream, dream-reader
vision, dreamy; wishes

1

Crazy Dreams

Take my hand and be lead out of your time.
Pass sea breezes and over mountaintops.
Rest your heart free and fly over your own land.
See your wishes come true rather than pass.
We need not let go of our first thought and dreams.
We need not listen to those so mean.
You need not a map to lead your way.
You need not a person to make your day.
Just rest upon the dreams you carried so deep
As a child.
The dreams you lost along the way, because all
around was so loud.
It's still there, still possible, still in your reach.
Remember in the beginning, no one was there
To teach.
You made your dreams all by yourself.
You based it on your wishes all by yourself.
Over days and nights they may have changed shape.
Over months and years, making you think it's
A mistake.
As the clock ticks on and you don't live out your life,
finding yourself in the end, bitter as a knife.
Why should it be? Why let your dreams go?
Know from the beginning your dreams were all,
You know.
So I guess it's safe to say your crazy dreams you
must take. If you don't, in the end you'll find it
Was a mistake.

So dream

Sandman

Time passing,
Tears rolling over sea and land, from the eyes
Of one with heart and soul.
God's child walking this earth.
Holding onto sunshine's and dandy-lions.
The simple scent of air is enough to fill this
One's day with thanks to breathe.
Caring is a responsibility not taken by all so easy.
Some stagger and hide, while others open and
embrace a chance to help.
We try to learn from all those stars before us and
walk around the holes left behind by those that
were not able to see in time.
Passing the trail of blood and tears thinking,
Oh, what it must have been to be just too late,
Or not at all.
We hope all is well tomorrow after the storm passes.
We are willing to help lift the spirits of those
God's children.
We will share song and food,
Listen to the words dying to be heard, and
Rub the back till they all fall silently asleep in a
dream of better days.
Then and only then will we leave our post for,
At that time we will know that there is no more
We can offer and the sandman will finish the job
As they all sleep softly through the night.

Dreams

*Now is the time to wonder if there
Can be such a thing as a dream?
Seems like the time can take all
Feelings from it,
Causing one to remember yesterday,
Looking out of your own childhood eyes,
Wondering if it ever was more than just a dream?*

View of Love

We walk this earth with eyes filled from
Realizing that dreams hardly come true.
We try to keep our head high and maintain
Our own greatness as we go but, after time
And disappointment from seeing nothing
Change around you, you become discouraged
And lose some of the greatness that's kept
Your soul warm.
Being who we are, we don't give up the things
We know and keep dear to our hearts.
Love has always been at the top of our list
And for so long we have fought to hold onto
These dreams. There have been so many people
And things that have come our way and tried
To convince us that the way the world views
This great power love, is the way.
Well, I just see something else and would rather
Live without.

Signed,
Love at 1st sight

I had a dream

I had a dream.
Flower laid roads and sweet honey kisses
From someone with love in their heart and
Patience in mind.
I had a dream of playing with my dog at the beach,
My kids running round as I held the hand of my love
And walked in the sand.
I had a dream of time passing and I,
Pulling up the fresh veggies from my yard.
Picking ripe plums from my tree so sweet,
And lying back with the sun on my brow.
I had a dream of hearing waves rolling
Across the horizon,
Splashing into a rainbow of mist
That brushed and cooled my face.
I had a dream about being in love
With someone that loved me 2.
I had a dream of a peaceful land where people
Treated each other with kindness and respect,
Where children were happy with the day and
Thought how they could grow to be great.
I had a dream of crying from being so happy,
Rather than crying from being so sad.

I had a dream.

A Gift

Art's first in my life.
It is the essence of my birth
and the red in my blood.
Much and many has tried to
drown out this light but has failed.
I have lost friend, money and women
on my journey but never a tear
for my path is clear.
What rewards await at the end
of my days are untold as well as unknown.
At times there are none that can
even explain why I do as I do
and am willing to sacrifice even
life in my pursuit to surrender
my all with nothing more.
I am man and this is my truth.
I only wish to be lead towards
the path that I am destine to walk.
Along my way I will forever share
this gift extended to me for
I do understand that apart of this
gift is also for you.
May it strengthen you as you cry
and help you remember your own
soul as you walk through the life
and it reveals your truth to you.

Best'em Join'em

Stretching out your arms to this world.
Walking with open heart and mind
Through a plush field of hope and promise.
Believing in your heart, knowing it won't
Lead you into danger if you only believe.
Closing your eyes to the masses dictation
And action. Following your private quest to
Eden, remembering those Hollywood
Stories like, West Side Story, My Fair Lady
And Romeo and Juliet.
Closing your eyes to the rest and living
In that silver screen of make believe love.
Knowing in your heart that it's all real.
What happens to those dreamers when they
Awaken to the sounds of cars and loud voices?
What happens when they push you off your
Cloud into reality?
Can you really blame another, or were you just
The fool for believing in what you wanted to believe?
Where do you go from there?
You can't beat them so must you join them?
You! Knowing there's no place to hide but,
you can't join the masses.
You just can't!
So what!
Where's your home?
Is the only safe place in death, in the arms of
Our Lord or do you just join the masses and
Give up on love?
God forbid

Run and Hide

So what do I do now?
Do I run like a deer, leaping over all trying
To hide from the man with their big gun.
Do I act as man and prepare myself to be spilled
And wasted for no reason at all.
Is it safe, is what my tears are filled with.
Can I just be me and in doing so,
Will they be able to find appreciation,
For this man I am?
The big world with its monsters running about
Trying their best to take my soul and break my
Heart for senseless reasons that I will never
Deserve for I will never offer nothing more than
Truth while wishing only love.
Can I just be me and you find that within me
lies many sunny days.
Let me keep my happy world.
I believe in the love even if it's so hard to see.
You were brought to me by an angel I say,
For I can not understand any other way you
Could have got here.
So, welcome.
I hope that you find safety in my heart
And wish me bestdays as I for you.

All will be

Close your eyes and feel me there.
In heart and soul, release your rhythm
To mine and over time all will be.
Feel it for it is there.
It may seem cold but,
In heart this could never be.
So know this as you sleep and
May your slumber be forever sweet.

With love

Out there

*I know that you can hear me
As you pass life out there.
I still can see you in my dream,
playing with my hair.
All that was left was a picture
Of you hanging on the wall.
All that was left was a picture
And it said it all.*

*Life
n life; remain alive,
bustle, call into being;
alive, lifelong -
life&death, lifesaver.*

2

Beauty within Beast

Seeing beauty within beast,
Fear over stars that shine brighter.
Wonders untold and sometimes forgotten.
Love me not and say me no friend.
Waters choppy and currents tossed.
One sign is all that's needed to understand
The way. If you get lost, you can always
Follow the moon towards north and the
Milky Way.
Forever smile on your journey and see
The sun as she sets.
Wonderful wonderful life awaits you and
Your grace. You are truly a wonder that
Your mother can be proud of and
No one can ever take your place.

So remember...

In touch

In touch, in touching people.
Souls lost over long days
With sweat to hold us silent.
Wonderful music to soothe our
Minds and remember dreams
Lost along the way.
You are a star!
Didn't your mama tell you that.
Questions put forth, in front
Of your face to see into tomorrow,
Rather than getting caught
Up in it.
You can smile and rush if you like.
Your works are working and you
Don't even know it. Jumping the gun,
Landing to see it still sitting there, staring
You right in the face.
Mad, mad world, you know the rules…
So only accept the life as it accepts you.
Stagger not, want not, need not, for
It is all there up close and personal.
You must only believe in your works
In order for them to live upon our earth.
Daily chores are required to assist in
The natural process so you may
Understand things that are presented.
Accept all challenges without fear or un-comfort.
Your sweet music will ring as long as you
Are able to hear yourself,
your heart, your dream,
Forever

Blown

Set adrift upon a stream,
Blown in which ever direction
The wind decides to go.
Will I be blown into a storm
That will toss me without
Mercy and crash I against
The rocks? Will the rain beat
My face red and disguise the
Tears rolling down my cheeks.
Will I be washed ashore, left in
A barren land alone or will we
Be swept away to calm water.
Her clear blue revealing all her
Wonders below. To bathe in her depth,
In her wet soul knowing nothing
But her sound and the wet kiss
She left on our cheek.
Which way will we be blown
And how clean will we be when
All is done?

Directions

A road, a trail, a path we walk.
Leaving traces of memories from good, from bad.
Some stop to cry.
Some stop to talk.
Some stop just to think about what they had.
Most memories remain by one's side till death.
Some leave us limp, not knowing what's next.
Why do we keep walking further away from
Those thoughts?
Why don't we stop,
Turn round rather than blowing it off?
Maybe memories are too scary to see up close.
Maybe memories remind us of ourselves the most.
Looking through a looking glass, look at yourself,
Remembering yesterday, seeing it as a ghost.
I guess those roads, that trail,
Will forever lead back to you.
I guess the memories will forever
Be a dictionary of you.

Mommy

So now I see how Mommy must of felt, hoeing for bread to feed her three children. Going door to door, getting that no, as a response over and over again. Pounding the asphalt day after day, looking for one chance to sleep knowing her children are safe
And warm.
Stress red, thinking of how she will feed
Them tomorrow.
How will she fill the tree at Christmas?
How will she keep the lights on and if she can make a cake on our birthday,
Will she be able to get enough candles to add up
The years.
Looking to God for help.
Looking to the heavens for answers.
Hearing that voice in the background, telling her to be strong and don't give up for everything will work itself out in time.
Believing in things unrevealed to her, then drowning herself in liquor or untrue loves so she won't see the reality lived.
So happy when one offered even the smallest help
For every little bit counted so much. Then in the Background of this struggle, the faint reminds that was told to her when she was without child,
When she was a little girl.
Those words telling her she was beautiful, she would grow to be great, that she could fly and how could she forget this?
How could she open her eyes to find that her own Mother offered nothing but lies.
That in reality she would feel the bitter streets and

*give away her womanhood for a Mr. Goodbar, that
Prince Charming was really a pimp that rode a
Cadillac and that he would not beat dragons but,
Her in the end,
That Mothers Day was actually the only day she
would see a golden pot in the form of a welfare
Check from the government.
I can only wonder if before life was granted,
If she choose hers?
Did I choose mine and if so, why?
What is the purpose of it all? Must our struggle be so,
so our child's is not?
So our child's, child is not and then in most cases,
that is not even so.
One can only wonder if we ever had a choice at all,
for it's hard to believe that we would have chosen
such a long way around.
I stand now looking at it all with eyes and heart full
of tears for us both.
For my mother, I will pick up where she left off and
for her I promise that I will change this nasty river
Of tears to one of clear blue, warm waters that she
can bathe in forever.
For if she was forced to suffer and struggle so much
for the sake of her child, then as her child,
I will repay the debt.*

*Made with Love,
Mommy*

Sweet Dreams

And who says yea or nea,
Who cries after the war and
Who sings when the sun rises?
Drifting on yesterday's current,
Swaying about with wonders
Of, only if I's.
Now the sun sets upon dandelions,
Putting them to sleep just so they
Can wake to brighter days tomorrow.
Sweet, Sweet Ocean blue, spraying
My face with cool breezes of love me not's
And big kisses from one's heart.
Thank you for u and may you
Forever wake to the sun in your hair.

Goodnight

Tick Toc

Tick Toc, Tick Toc
Shoot, look at the time pass.
You're all gray.
Look at yourself holding on for dear life.
What happened to you?
Forgotten with time and turned to tears and anger.
Each point standing over the other,
Drowning out the other.
Cursing and pissing over everything in sight!
Disney said," Happily ever after"
The end.
Must I only have fairytales
Of make believe to believe in?
Is it the safest road the life will lay?
Is this the little spot I
Must sit on for dreams of grandeur?
And of love,
Is it love?
A war I could never win
Without the heart of the pure.
Tomorrow will be here soon.
Will I live to carry the pail from the stream
Just to see the hole in the bottom and fill it
Again and again?
Will the wicked and cold, thy hearts
Ever cry out for love and caring or
Will this only come after they wake up
From the dream they call beautiful?

Bgood

Who is the one that decides if you were
Great in your life?
Is it God, your mother, maybe your friends?
Maybe it all comes back to you, and you're
Deepest beliefs of life itself?
To be great in the life you lead must be
A wonderful feeling when it's all done.
To sit back on those clouds and see children
Follow the ways you left behind.
To see the glee in their faces when they understand
that it is possible to see themselves become great too.

For me, that is a great life.

Letter to Life

Forget you, you deceiver.
The fake messiah that we deal with daily.
Teasing us with fruit and fantasy.
Examples from corpses long ago
Lost and unappreciated until death.
Even children are not spared and
Murphy's Law, out ways any chance
For simple peace.
To always know nothing ever last
And hope is the only light one can truly have.
Forget you life,
For my own child should not be born to
Serve your will and our ancestors before
Should have been rewarded rather than raped.
Art, an outlet blessed,
All caged like an animal and replaced
With dollar signs that make you choose
To let go of your brush,
Rather than paint the world in colors from our soul.
Forget you life,
For even challenging our one true savior, love.
For making even her sweetness beg for mercy.
I find no explanation for this test of time
And I fear the answers will only reveal thyself
In death.

Waiting, waiting, waiting for answers.

Artist

Real All The Time

Taking over the pen from thy that's
Spouted out so many words of rules
And regulations over the land thy stand on.
Strange that the words have a hard time
Flowing when you don't have your protective
Phone to hide behind like a sniper in the bush.
Today to remember one's own yesterday,
Is to take a step towards growth and wisdom.
A bird that can't fly dies in a cage.
The player that has no one to play with
Is on unfamiliar ground.
The fake messiah that blows balls of fire
Out their mouth is truly a fake messiah
And one that lies to his own heart is a fool.

Enough

So what is the reason for all this madness?
Have I not given up enough ass for you?
Have I not toiled and turned my back
Towards the obvious wrongs and if so why
Must punishment be cast down daily?
Visions of nightmares brought to life, ever so near.
Understanding has lost meaning and anger starts to
Creep in for it is more justice than what is
Being served today and yesterday.
Yes, I know that I am suppose to just say,
"Cool" and keep climbing but, what if I'm
Tired of this madness and wish it not anymore!
Can I at least be told the reason behind
This suffering. Can't I at least know why
I must be chosen to die an awful death?

*Some understand,
And some just don't.*

Here is a Place

Here is a place.
It's soft so we can feel the cool breeze drift over the ocean to our face.
So warm and comforting like your mother's breast.
Loving the day because if you don't, you'll cry.
Thinking of tomorrow and the day you'll die.
Give us a smile to help remind us of the fun around.
Playing and knowing that you are the one,
Not a clown.
Some can't see cause, they choose to be blind.
Can't see or say because you may have to lie.
They should look anyway, even if it makes them cry.
Although it's hard to do, you must be real.
To go through tomorrow,
To teach your children to deal.
Can't say what happened,
Don't remember the road.
We've must of missed it somewhere.
Maybe you were too busy crying,
From all the lie's you've been told?
We feel like we've tried and are all puckered out.
We want to die
And fly,
Then scream and shout.
Maybe all we have to look for is a bottle and a gun.
I just hope in the end,
The better of you is passed on to my son.
Never should have been here in the first place!

Auntie

Dear Auntie,

    Sad to say that this is the first time I wrote you a letter. I guess I should start by saying sorry for that, knowing now that I will never have an address to forward it to or that I could of yesterday.
    Well, I hope you're fine in heaven and understand that I really love you and everything you were about. You really helped me believe, regardless of how dark it may seem. You taught me to pray, which is a gift that none through time could ever top.
    Auntie, I will miss you and will try to remember and practice all the wonderful things you taught me. I also hope you like the music side of me. I really wanted to share that with you and wanted to know what you thought and if you liked it. Well, I hope you get this letter even if I don't have a address for forwarding.

Love you Auntie

America

*Listen to the patter of footsteps passing along
The streets of America.
The sun shinning on the asphalt and peoples
Dreams are soothed by the image in the air.
Exciting from understanding that all is possible.
From wealth to poverty, from homes surrounded
By picket fences and cars of all shapes, colors
And sizes.
And that sound and smell of newborn around.
I hear the cry's of new mothers that are just
learning forever. Oh, what a gift our America,
So much and still so cold. We truly have it all.
It is a bother to see we have not been able to
completely throw down those ways that have
Long ago proven so wrong. Brothers still killing
brothers and boxes made of empty dreams from
Birth and renamed.
Senseless Murder is what I call it.
Although I know it's not too late, I still sigh for
It is still way overdue.
We go on with heads high still proud of what we
choose to do, as long as we, never wish harm,
We will always be able to go on.
So thank you America.*

No words

So I killed the poem.
Let it bleed in the street.

Did not give a damn if it
Drop them all to their feet.

Don't even know my name.
So how could they care?

Leave me in the snow to die,
For I have no fear.

The end is supposed to come sooner or later.
So what am I waiting for?

Poetry in Motion
2001NN Train Berlin

No answers

Gotta stop lying to myself right here and now!
Be real about everything sitting up so close
in your face.
Be the man I am and see that truck coming
and avoid it.
Gotta stop listening to my own lying heart,
clouding my mind and confusing my every move.
Gotta grow and learn to read the signs and let
them help shine the way in the dark.
Help warm the reminds of my own soul.
The signs are helpful even if they're sad at times
but, it's all a part of the life.
These things, if we can see,
Good and bad are all a part of the life.
I'm sure I will feel better after I understand more.
I'm not scared. I have walked
and seen more dangers than one should.
I have been groomed and remember.
How else will I know that truck is coming?
How will I avoid that stray bullet,
whistling from 84th street.?
Yes, it's true my emotions run deep
and I cry for the world and don't think we as
a people are helping in its growth and happiness.
For those that are too busy to shed a tear,
to stop, turn around and help,
They are the ones ruling the world
and running it down.
Oh, what anger runs over me,
over questions for tomorrow.
I guess to think of my babies' challenges are enough.
Then again there's no rule book besides
the same life we all must live.

Everybody playing Lotto, in search of that pot
of gold that's to die for.
At least in the end the donkey gets to eat the
carrot after he let John ride his back up and
down that hill.
Lotto can be hope though and for most,
that's all that's needed and more.
For me I just can't or don't want to
Believe that this is it.
I don't believe and won't get in line with
the others marching down their plastic streets.
And if I did, I would at least remember
how to have a heart.

Heart

Heart
['heart] a fig. courage -
spirit; take heart - whole-
heartedly; heart's desire,
heartless, heartattack

3

Keep the faith

Saving the world.
Saving men from themselves.
Looking them straight in the eye,
Seeing clearly that we all need help.
Feeling like a chosen one,
Put here to set them free,
Understanding the sacrifice.
It may even kill me.
Pulled away from my children.
Missing them everyday.
Praying, pleading and hoping
They are happy anyway.
Wishing for butterflies to pass them
Every step of their way.
Knowing that as they pass in flight,
This means that it is your lucky day.
Giving thanks for the angels specially sent for me.
Knowing that they help me on my way
When it is hard to see.
Every second the clock ticks,
We know we still have time.
Giving our all to make things better.
Then all will work out fine.
So many lost sheep scattered across the land.
Lost children, broken hearts and wars to make us cry.
Things look so black it truly is hard to know the way,
I guess that's why our mothers
Always taught us how to pray.
Keep the faith in your own dreams.
Give all of you everyday.
Never quit or give up.
Never listen to what others say.

Hold tight! Stand tall!
It will all come soon.
You just have to believe in your dreams.
If we give up this, then we're all doomed.
Keep the faith

Will Not Falter

*On stand by, waiting for the life to break me
Off a piece. Trusting in the nature to find me
Under the cloud the haters are trying to put
Around my sunshine.
Taking big steps and shooting bull's eyes across
The board. Destiny is mine so I live the day as
Any other but humble for I truly am tired and
Every step has become the harder.
Trust in God, as I believe in myself.
Without music today, without love from one.
Only visions that are clearer than the life that sits
In my face daily. Although I am fine with the wait,
I still feel the tears in my soul.
Knowing the life of yesterday and all the faces
I've had to leave behind. My mission is relentless
And leaves me tired and sometimes sad.
It's hard to understand why I am so and it's harder
To understand all that is lost in the process.
So, my tears are heavy and now thinking about it,
I guess it's mandatory in order for me to feel
And understand who I am and more.
So remember that I have a heart.
I know that I can do everything that's needed
Around the world to make it better but,
It's sort of o.k. just because I know I am
Also not alone in my desire.
So I will be the solider I am and march
Forward with my head held high.
I will do my part and live it till I have
Not another breath within me so,
I am patient for this and will not falter.*

Go on

Not so sure about tomorrow but
I'm gonna go on!
May seem unclear today
So we must be strong.

Not sure about tomorrow but
I'm Gonna go on on.
I did not just come here
To turn and go home.

May get a mountain
Thrown right in my face.
May lose all my life and friends
That I thought was o.k.
But, I have to go on,
On my own way
My way,
My way,
Regardless of what they say.
My way

New born

So the test is at hand. The big macaroni.
No lies, no liars, no shame.
Only real artist are recognized in this land
We call America. The rewards are great if
You are accepted by those critics that sit
High on a platinum chair.
The decision makers that have the power
To spread your words around the world.
The man that can easily spread your gift
Globally around and this is exactly what's
Needed for the world to be freed and for
You/me to live as we were born to do.
The problem is that all those that are invited
Into the world of greatness that have positive
Actions are killed at an early beginning and the
Demons are sleepless working to keep us from
Our way. To keep us from opening the eyes of
Man and child. The man wants dirty words to
Fill our streets and for our children to kill each other,
spit in our mother's eye and leave new borns
In a wastebasket to die. And then there is hope,
Aloha at the end of the line. They're alone,
With tears streaming down their cheeks and
Empty pockets. Those in front stand clear from the
smell of freshness, from the sight of goodness, from
The message that is printed on their forehead.
All around frown and bad name this sweetness
Of flower. The only ones that can see clear of this
slander are children that are truly powerless.
Children that can only raise enough strength to
Crawl to their mothers and weep from what they see,
from what they can't change, from this mother more

*scary than an open closet in the dark.
Then by the time these children are well enough
To stand, they already have been stripped of the way
And have merely joined in the mass hysteria of
Man's wrongful steps.
So I ask, how can we win without weapons?
How can we get pass the man in the platinum chair
without losing our childhood eyes?
I have not an answer yet and today I will cry
From seeing the struggle ahead.
Today I will cry for it is a part of the journey but,
Just because tears fall, it does not mean that hope
Is lost and it does not, does not mean,
I will fail.*

Space

Regardless of time and space there must
Still be enough room for us.
Our own air and space away from it all.
Above our mates and parents time.
Just a sanctuary for our own room
To release individual tears without restriction,
without care of the other ways taught by other man.
Just a place to grow.

Passing Judgment

What can you say?
Every man seems to pass judgment on my part.
Every woman is ready to tell me the road that's
Best for me. Frowning their faces and looking
Down upon me because they believe to know
A better way.
Rolling their eyes and breathing under their breath.
Shame of my company cause they believe I'm
So wrong. Do you think they have a better plan or
Do they think they have a better plan?
Deaf to your words and dumb to your actions.
Hanging around you because they feel pity,
Not love. Sorrow, not respect.
I can see these men walking around me with their
big signs of, " I'm better than thy or there is
better than you"! Compete with me or the rest of
You is a game.
I don't want to play.
I would rather be looked at by the dumb as if I'm
The same. I have nothing to prove to you or the next.
I can be myself, not you or Tom.
If you see the world's offerings and yearn for what
You don't have, go after it, find it, love it, cherish it
and be happy.
Don't try to save me as you hang-out and say,
"I tried". Don't settle for less if you need more.
This road can only come to an end for looking down
at me and scrutinizing my every movement while I
try to satisfy this world still giving no understanding.
I see a mold that I can't line up to in your eyes.
You're looking at me with your judgment then
looking upon thyself and are blind.

I can't win here, Never a man.
Just something to talk about or look at and say,
"I know of better men".
I say, find a better man than I! Eat him apart. Believe
in and love him to death, or until you decide he's really
nothing as well.
Always look at yourself and change nothing then
look at the world and try to change it all.
A person like this can never be satisfied for their
Eyes will run under the table when the mirror is
placed in eyes view but, still forever ready to judge
someone else's reflection.
So how can one live up to a God anyway?

Good vs. Bad

Take off that mask so I can see your face.
Dead eye, up on you. Tight as a bow.
Unafraid of uncertainty because I know my way.
Come down lion, for I am ready and you are
No challenge for my truth and as time passes,
You shall slowly turn to dust and be blown across
The winds of forgotten, while my truth streaks
To the top of the sky and above forever.
There are only two roads that are offered
When we come. Your decision need be clearly exact,
For you are judged at the highest and all your worth
will be tested.
Be ready my friend. Your time is little compared
To your actions.
What will you decide in your forever?
How will you speak when the only one that is
listening is you.
Good vs. Bad, so simple when spelled out on paper.
Who are you under these guides?
What is your measure when no one sees but you
And then we have life to help us lose sight of death.
If there be one rule book to help us on this quest,
We need her dearly and if only some words to offer
To save, It must be, choose wisely.

Art surrounds

So think, this fog lingering overhead.
I can feel the chill raise bumps upon my arm.
Surrounded by the art coming out of me and
By strangers that carry gifts of their own.
Some walk as if they are apart but the true ones
clearly see who does not belong.
Taken out of the game by faith not choice.
Art surrounds you freely if you truly are an Artist.
All soldiers marching into battle with peace and
music, acting as gun to protect and stand up till
Death for the art in its purest form.
No wonder we wish all and everyone love, for the
two go hand and hand and this could never be
separated no matter how much one may try.
Love and Art, brother and sister to each other,
Kin bounded by community, by love, by Art.
We worriers are tired from the journey but we still
stand tall and will forever have more room to
make more happen, till death do we part.

Winter is Coming

Sweet scents lifting up from the spring flowers
In bloom. Sunbeams reaching out to all.
Helping with the master plan of growth.
Some cold days and some rainy,
Just To feed goose bumps.
Do you remember when you kissed me in the
Sand as the sun went down and how it tingled so?
Do you remember those cold nights?
Me warming your all merely with my bodies
Touch close to yours?
Do you remember what the fall leaves looked
Like last year, when we made love and will
That fall love, ever live again in our today?
Winter is coming and I fear it will be cold.
I can only wish the love will withstand
And you remember this warmth I give.

A day Without

What is a day without love within?
Can one say the sun will shine so bright?
Will the drops of rain feel so soft upon
Hitting thy cheek?
How will the moon shine so bright a path
lies clear, leading a way to the next place.
Will one be able to smile when they see a
Child take its first steps?
I wonder just how different the life would be
without love, and pray we never have to find out.

4me a day without love,
Is a life without meaning.

Let's Make Something Beautiful.

So Maybe It's Not Me

So Maybe it's not me.
Maybe I am the clear one in my house.
I can see flowers scents rise to the
Heavens and smile from it.
I can love deep and cry over
Some old black and white movie
That I have seen a million times.
I can look the bigger man in the eye
And tell them that I am a better man.
I can raise children without their mother
And help them to always know, they are loved.
I can sing a song from the top
Of my head and make you cry.
I can write my words with expression
And not worry about what they think.
I can be alone and not try to push the
Obvious for I know it will come when it's time.
So maybe it's not me for I am not afraid
To love even If my heart has been broken.
I can go to Disneyland and have as much fun
As any child, although I myself, may be gray.
I can turn and walk away if those around
Have proven to be of a way that is not
Becoming of me.
I can love all mankind regardless of colors
Or creed even if they do not love themselves or me.
I can forever appreciate the rain for I know
That it brings on flowers tomorrow.
So maybe it's not me.
Maybe it's the air of others
That have only forgotten their way.
For I remember...

Mine Mouth

Why do I spill out mine mouth,
Words I believed can help our
World in any way.
Knowing I am man as the rest.
None greater or weaker,
With no more love than that born
in my soul when I first breathe.
A man with the ability to speak,
To walk, to care.
Is my path and my heart so different
That I have the right to say and if so,
Is there one alive that can hear and
Understand my words?
I guess I must bear the answer to
My own questions and see the path
For my own way.
Along the trail, I only wish to share
And have the same offered in return.

No Dream

Air swirling around.
Too many years just blowing by.
Too little, too late, are words I wish never to hear again.
The movement has always been there waiting
To be picked up and placed in its proper place.
No more looks into someone else's yard.
No more wishes or prayers waiting to be heard.
Just air, my air I share with none other
Than the child born by I.
Releasing myself from the elements around.
Hearing nothing but my own sound,
The blessed, the few.
I was not forgotten by man.
I was forgotten by myself.
Now the prize awaits I and no man or women
Or God will stop this divine right of me.

The Gardener

So dark,
I can't see my hands in front of my face.
Look at it all melt away into nothing.
To think of not being able to smell the
Flowers anymore kills the soul of the gardener,
For he has toiled the ground,
Watered and provided sun.
Only hoping the seed would grow into a wonderful
flower that would withstand the storm.
Now as he sits in the mud, crying over his own
flowerbed because the fear and reality is tearing
Him to shreds and no one, not no one,
Can hear his cry!

Save the gardener...

I am clear

Time passes, I'm growing.
Another train another view.
Loved ones near crying inside out.
Still fighting the life cause life's never lets up.
Never extending a moment to just eat up the air.
So numb my body,
Haunted by ghost that want to
Follow me and wish me bad.
No sleep tonight.
It's o.k. I am man.
I have the power to make a better way.
With my shield to repel the ways they
Throw at me to make me stop,
And my understanding that,
One can make a difference.
I shall live to my full worth as man,
As the truth holds,
Bestowed in me by my ancestors.
I am music!
She is my ancestor and she will be
The direct outlet for everyone.
I will ready myself for tomorrow
And cry when I must but without fear,
For I am clear.
Bless us on our way
And keep us from harm.

With love...

One's Imagination

Yo Bro.'
Another day that came 2go.
Who can judge one's imagination?
Taking the brush from our hand.
Trying to add the colors they think are best!
Who are they, those people that don't believe
That Luke did have the power!
Who are those wondering souls?
And where did they come from?

More Words

I can't hear you people
And you have so much to say.
Words used in another way.
Sharing with thy brother man,
Adding a different color to
Those that may hear.
What a gift to receive.
Words, words and more words
From me to you.

I Shall Sing

Wow, what a wonder to behold,
The life with all it's flavors.
So similar and at the same time,
So different.
To sit stage side for the thousandth time
Of my life and feel this floor beneath
My feet are beyond this air I breathe.
I have felt this floor for so long and have
Heard its cry long ago for my song.
Now I hear the message oh too clear
And I have known this from the start.
Regardless of time, words of others
That wish me stop. Regardless of the
Strokes that scare my heart till death,
Now I will follow the message that
Cries from all stages round our world.
I shall sing...

Sticks and Stones

And today I've seen clear
The sticks thrown my way.
I could easily see fire in my
Brother man's eye who know me not.
Wish you better dead,
Is what was so easily read in the air
And then the pull.
So easy to just join in and feed their way.
Never!

Easy

Why can't it be easy?
Must life forever be hard?
Can we just love one another,
Understanding it's nothing to discard?
Can't love find its way even if in the dark?
Can't people be gentle to each other,
Flying free as a Lark?
Is it really the life that's hard
Or is it maybe you?
Maybe your eyes are closed
And you don't see what you do?
If we all lend a hand,
Maybe it would be easier to see
Just how wonderful life is,
For you and for me.
One man can change the world,
So my friend let's start with you,
For in the end, it's easier,
Before we all are through.

Fly

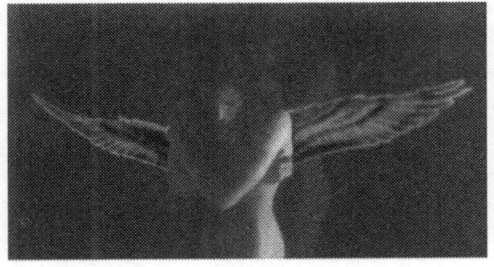

*Fly
['fly] fly weight;
airman; birds,
dream state;
(to be in) love*

4

Angels

And long ago, there were two angels born upon Our world. As friends they played, flying about, granting wishes to those that needed them most. When storms came, they sheltered each other as friends in love do.

One day as the summer sun shined bright, they found that their friendship bloomed into love and appreciation and in the end all they could do was extend each other a kiss that lasted forever.

Sun Beams

Sun beams to light a path
Where one can walk on in glee.
Flowers aligning the way
To a place of love that's free.
Challenged by obstacles
That may have been laid along the way.
Rainy days and tragedies,
To try to convince you to go away.
Tears can fall from your eyes if
You do not know your way.
You have to see what you are here for
And live your life in no other way.
Dreams are not just this that blow away.
When you rise out of bed,
They definitely are a part of you
So, you should listen to what you said.
Don't get caught up in the life
And give it all away.
Make sure you give some back to you,
For you need it to be happy.
Add some of your sugar around your day,
To make it sweet as can be.
You as an individual have wonders,
Wonders we want to see.
Follow that sunbeam,
It can't be made clearer you see,
You my friend as you,
You have to be as you're suppose to be.
Happy
Happy
Happy,
So be...

Be proud

Be proud of the things you do
Because it's all of you.
If you want you can fly to the stars one way.

Be proud of your steps,
Need not listen what they say,
As long as it makes you,
Takes you to a place happy.

Be proud of the things you do
Because it's all of you,
You need you in the end you see.

Be proud my brother man because
Your mother told you too,
Need not cry or feel shame.

Be proud of what you do.
Be proud

Fly'in

Just look in my eyes.
Can't you see it overflow
and out?
Control it, contain it, ignore it.
Not poss!
You see,
it can't be stopped.
Look back and fall deep into this.

Fly'in with me,
Just fly'in,
Just fly'in.
Let yourself go and come.
It will spread like wings to lift
U up, and above the clouds.
Fly'in high on nothing but,

LOVE.

No Journal

Let me tip my glass to you, fair world.
In honor of the glorious way you throw
Things around. Forget it!
This child so young and pure must die.
Love has to be such a game of ticktacktoe,
Where no one wins.
We need wars and non-thought of killings
Because some old map proclaims this land is ours.
Oh, how we've twisted life into a mess.
Full of answers not thought through.
Full of ways we can only think is right.
If we man so wise, why is there only the bible
To lead us clear? How come no new journal has
Been kept to help God's own blessed children?
We only hope the ones we know will live long
Enough to share the wisdom, directing us
Away from harms way.
May God bless.

The Buffalo

Don't forget your path, crazy boy.
Feel and remember the buffalo that
Saved your kin with its fur in winter,
And meat for our tribe.
Screaming top the mountains your name
    Keno...
Feel the eagle's third eye look itself in the mirror.
Sore across your dreams and face the rest with Aloha.
The blood has spilled upon our streets
And we remember not.
We can still walk over the
Numbness, that's left to feel.
Remember the White Buffalo!
Yours forever, you whom you come
With into this world of questions.
One love,
One survival,
One family.
Today, to shine as the sun,
Is to fly beyond our own spirit and mind.
Trying to touch God,
While feeling helpless to the wind.
Blow away the dark clouds and give me
The strength to neutralize them all.
Forever sunshine and God bless the buffalo.

In God We Trust

What are words without meaning?
What is love without love, love more,
And what is life without flowers in spring?
Life is life and nothing more should be expected.
Unfortunately life's cruel,
So what comes is not enough.
Maybe some have food and can't understand
Why others may be hungry.
Some have dreams,
So they can't spell nightmare for trying.
Whatever one has verses another should
Matter little if there's an understanding that
All deserves no more or less than the other.
Understanding for your bread'ren,
Comfort, for your friend.
A huge for your love,
Or just words from with-in.
In God we trust.
Some gifts are small,
But carry much weight.
Those little things we forget,
God knows it's a mistake.
I guess the worst is to love,
But not to be able to love more.
Yourself open-ended just to do the day,
Rather than living and fully loving that day.
You can say, one man's diary, is another
mans scribble, but one man's love, is all that
One can love.
Till your time comes when you can
Experience such a wonder,
It may be hard to understand these words,
But still possible to feel it's thunder.

Prosperity

So sweet this sea, the freshness in the air.
Children running about, with no type of fear.
So loud, their voices of pure joy even if it
Be just for that moment.
Everyone knows dreams.
All know that they and their child have a
Chance to be great upon this planet.
It is hard but not so hard.
In between, the life is enjoyed in the form of
Birth and family prosperity.
There are many obstacles put up close to see.
Temptation, fear and love wars are enough to
Make one lose their way and many already have.
It's hard to say that there are not so many happy
Children around me without lead homes.
If this was other, I doubt their voices of laughter
Would be so strong.
It is much easier to think there will be a lot
Of children sleeping tight tonight from their
Day at Alameda Beach.

Poetry End

For the poetry in our hearts, a force
That could not be stopped.
Not forced, not made, not given, our taken.
Merely expressed through words of truth,
For music in song.

Tomorrow will forever be tomorrow
And we shall always do as we grow.

Poetry in song, uniting worlds and out bursting
Into our soft air we breathe.
Forever soul mate, I know I have found
And this for me and mine alike.
May we always hear her sound in words,
As we live our lives through.

Poetry in Motion 2001
NN Train Berlin

So Much Life

So much life in us all.
So much wonder within.
Release your essence
And feel yourself fly.

All answers inside of you.
You don't even have to try.

Regardless of the burdens
That may come your way.
If you look deep in your soul,
You will always see colors so brilliant,
It can blind all those around, any day.

Your own special you.
Always wear it proud.

If you're sad then sing.
It will make you feel good.

If you're lost, then look deeper.
You'll find it within your
Own soul, as you should.

So much life, in all of us.
So much wonder within.
In your heart, you should trust.
Release your essence to fly away my friend.

Stuck in place

Stuck in place, in time,
Air none but still walking forward.
Knowing what tomorrow will bring
As long as I have faith and believe.

Cold at night,
Running though the day Non-stop,
Even missing water wells out of
Forgetfulness but still fueled to go on.

Pretty pictures along the way to remind and push
more but worthless unless there's closure within
Soul and fireflies forever giving the smallest light
While leading the way.

Remembering that we can cut the journey shorter
And just fly to our next stop, set up shop, sleep for
A spell and then wake to forever.

Tell me if someone knows, for I don't...

The life is truly the life so in it we breathe.
If man puts a stupid price on that air,
He himself has forgotten his own place
On our planet and may end up in the end with none.

Save us with enlightenment,
Educate our masses on how to take care so
We all may have just enough air to breathe.
Don't miss the signs

Mother's mother's mother

The light flows into you and you breathe life within,
from within, you breathe.
Eating life up like candy given to one that never
tasted sweet before.
From within or out.
Driving always without fail.
Cold, hot, rich, tired, you go.
Inner lights filling your action to move upon the
Day that was given to you as a gift, as one that
Was given life and lived.
So lucky you, getting that offering that was
Kindling down over time and unselfishly.
Who would know that that light would become a
child that learned to speak and walk and breathe.
Who would think that that light would become you.
This is fact for your mother's mother's mother said so.
At times hard to believe that we are that light that
Was made whole from an origin of love in
Some form, that this gift is more than most have
received and are probably left in some quiet part
Of our universe as merely a star and who can say
That is so bad?
It seems that we, in our form have lost the magic
That was given in gift, in love, in story.
There is still our mother's mother's mother
To prove anything less wrong.
Keep the faith, is what my friends mother told me.
I could tell from the love and understanding of
Life in her voice, that these words meant a lot
More than just words. There was just pure truth
In every part of the feeling that flowed out
Of her words. The crack in her voice, full of

*Pains and understanding, for time has revealed
Much and you could see it in her grown sons,
That grew in many.
So I heard this gift that came in the form of
Words from one that just knew.
Keep the faith and if you lose sight of it,
Take your woes to the cross and leave it there.
We breathe and if we are able to feel the earth spin
when hummingbirds take flight, we cry.
The rest is a free magic that we lost on the way.
Daily, effortless madness presented without
Warning or notice.
Damn, we are hard, us humans able to survive
dinosaurs and all.
Aren't we smart?
No, it's just that we have gifts that are on the level of
divine right but, it is still used in such a way that it is
hard to be proud of our humanity, our greatness.
Just look around. What do you see?
How is the gift being used and are we using it up?
Believe again, it's for our own good.
It will bring food tomorrow for the child unborn
And make us whole.
Love, love more.
How easy could it be?
Love, love more, the force to set us free.
You, me.
You, me,
You me
Love, love more*

Nothing...

Start here, I can't, perhaps I can.
This is not fair.
No! Stop it.
No words can find my words to explain.
Just look into my eyes,
Beyond what your eyes see.
I have smiles for you.
I love you.
Forever, I said forever!
Exactly.
No, don't write this.
No!
Now you really have to read between
The lines of my eyes.
I think it's sometimes difficult because
You're always asking.
What?
But sometimes the most beautiful
Thing is to look into your eyes and
Just say nothing...

Did u no

What do you have to say my friends about tomorrow?
Do you lie to yourself when you look in the mirror,
Still living life like it's a show?
Do you even know we all have the
Power to make a difference?
Do you even know we all must try to be clear,
With love and clear this funky air?

As a man we have the power to change much.

See Ya

*So now she tells me how nice the man is
that sits next to her. She says, he's nice because
he says Nothing about the loud, hard words
she so easily throws at me over the phone.
As she says this, she looks at him so he can
see and hear really what she thinks of her man.
She lets him know that she thinks nothing of
him as she hangs up the phone and goes to do her do.
Don't you know me and all the awareness
I have given to me from our lord?
Then you even are so bold to tell me
that I have not met your demands.
Demands, who in the hell do you think
you are to demand anything from me?
To think you have the power you were given
yesterday is only a fantasy in your mind.
You abused the privilege and abused me
because of your senseless habits so please,
check yourself!
Open your eyes instead of your mouth for once
and see that you control me no more.
You will never change, this is clear to me now
and I will never accept the wrongs of yesterday.
The good point here is that I'm sure
there are millions of people out there as senseless
as you and it will be easy for you to find a match
to appreciate you wholly in your land.
Till then save it for your friends
For I am not even this anymore.
Easy*

Soulmate

Sweet soulmate, I have found.
Unbelievable, scary, wonderful and true.
The road has been long and I even almost
Gave up on my dream of ever finding you.
I have given myself to so many over time,
Finding disappointment in the end.
Heart broken because I was wrong
Over and over again.
In the big world among people that disguised
themselves as friends and women that only wanted
My sex rather than my love.
Left to feel like a prostitute raped by life.
I am not that man that feeds off of women
And I am not that one that needs a night of lust,
waking in the morning to move onto the next.
Not I.
Since my childhood I always felt your soft kiss
In my dreams and heard your whisper in my ear.
To wait and believe that when the time is right
You would come.
I knew that the tears and pain of life would beat
Me down and that there was a great chance that
I would never see you in my lifetime.
Life's little tricks,
Testing our will,
Our strength and faith.
I knew it would be hard but, if I closed my eyes
To the world and followed my heart,
I would be lead to the one person
That would be by my side forever.
Now as I write a tear falls because
I think that after years, in my last hours,

*The heavens allowed me to press
My lips against the lips of my soulmate.
I drank with her. I smelled her. I laughed with her.
I held her. I looked in her eyes and asked her to bear
my child and then I told her, " I love you"
And she heard me.
Now another tear falls because then I had to fly away
and leave my soulmate that I have looked for for so
many years, behind to fight life without me.
First I could not understand how this could be so
But as I parted, I've seen that it is all a part of the
master plan and even if I feel ready to welcome you
into my life, that maybe you were not ready to come.
Just a little more time before forever could be
extended from both sides so, now I wait and pray
That I am not confused and that you hear the same
song in your heart.
Friend, mother, sister, lover, wife is what I see
In you. Love at first sight and I know my
Vision is clear.
Now even if I am on the other side of the world,
In reality I am by your side and I will never go away.
You are the other half of me and togetherness is
Our God given right.
Please do what you must in the time we are away
And ready yourself for forever. We are not perfect,
just human and I can only offer love and dedication
and a safe home full of wonderful dreams. I hope that
this is enough for you and you are eager to have me
in your arms again.
Soulmate is what I think of you and if you are
This one, follow your heart for it will lead you
Back to me soon.*

Still your flower

Am I still your flower?
Can we still play?
For in love that grows,
Skies may turn gray.
Yes, you are my love,
Spin me in circles till dizziness finds
Me reeling like my heart feels when
I see you through stained glass eyes.
You've taken my heart and
Put it in your little secret box.
Down at the bottom of your pocket,
Where years of lint have collected.
You can keep me there if you like.
It's nice and warm.
Just remember to let me breathe and
See the sunshine ever so often,
If I am still your flower.

Left Handed

Excuse me for me.
I have different directions and paths.
May seem awkward at first cause
I'm left-handed.
Matters not to the expressions you may
See me reveal after the storm when
You're still sitting in the eye of it all.
Why is there so much air but,
I still can not breathe?
And love...
My essence,
May never find my soul mate
or am I just so unfit for the job?
Happily ever After, I pray
while we just try to understand it all.

Who knows?

Love

*Love
['love] for love; for
the love of; 1. be in
love with; be fond of,
like 2.(be in) love*

5

Just Words

*Cherish the time you have with someone that
Loves you. Love is a special gift that is not
Found around any corner or under any rock.
Its life giving energy is more wonderful than
Our own wildest dreams or fantasies and when
You're lucky enough to have it enter your life,
You should really see it for what it's worth.
The time can give, but It can also take away.
Maybe it's hard to appreciate something when
It's there, but if it's gone, you may never get
The chance again to say,
I love you*

Just Words

Viva Amour

Which way does the moon turn when
Breezes from your heart, blows from within?
How can you find answers on the grains
Of sand that slipped through your fingers?
I love!
I breathe!
Sweeter is none over that first thought of love.
As tomorrow folds over yesterday's dreams.
The spot left on the wall from yesterday's tears.
I pray there is still love.
It's needed for all mankind.
Just to be able to love it and believe
With others, can help change the world.
Let it in!
Don't be scared.
Let it in!
While we live to learn,
We do to grow.
We're good to love
And we're bad to none.
I want to love.
I want to stay.
I just want to love,
No matter what you say!

Signed in love

Lovemenot

The tears that are pouring out of me for nothing.
This pain cutting my insides apart
Only because there's a knife on the table.
The struggle to breathe and eat just
To still gasp and go hungry.
The love running through my veins,
Uncared for and misunderstood.

Understand me not,
Think of me not,
Love me not.

How and Why

How and why the love so dear?
The pain I feel from my heart gone.
How and why will the sun ever shine again?
In the window and garden I held.
How and why should I take another step?
Be a good soldier and stand at attention
Without a smile or conscience,
Like them all,
Just knowing I must not leave my post,
For I am on guard but,
How and why should I take another step with
This hole bleeding straight through my heart,
With these people beating me down 'cause
They think they have it all,
But how and why do I fill this void?
I'm nothing to the next.
Why can't I just be myself
And loved for my wonders.
Why can't they see me? Why?
This will be an awful death to die without.
For once I've been worshiped just because of
The love I practice and carried dear to my soul.
It is a good thing, my love,
And if eyes would open, they will truly see
The most wonderful colors a person
Can or have ever seen, in me.
Till that day comes,
I shall slowly die a little at a time,
And hide my worth from them all.
So, how and why can flowers grow at all?

Love and Aloha

Love is a wonderful thing to experience,
And if you are lucky enough to feel that
Sweet poison warms your blood,
You truly have found a good reason to be happy.

Love and Aloha

Love Them

If love was the greatest thing on earth, why is it
That love is sharp as a knife that stabs the heart,
Rather than soothes?
Why is it so easy for someone that proclaims love,
To ill treat the one they proclaim it to?
To think that love gives you the right to hurt,
disrespect, lie to or not care for!
Is not the way love walks.
The steps formed into clouds leading to heaven,
disappearing from under your feet, falling to the solid
ground because your love cares not enough to hold
out their hand to catch your fall as they say,
" I LOVE YOU ",
Turn cheek, roll eyes and laugh in another's arms,
because your love has spoken their words of truth
that you can't stand, that you use against them
To push the knife in deeper
Than the life has already done.
Why care if tears roll down your lover's cheeks?
You love them right!
So why do you have to catch their fall too?
Why do you have to control your viciousness,
Your words of hate?
You love them and they need not know more.
Love is... Treating your love, less than love is?
No, this is not the love that flows from my fingertips,
and not the love I will ever believe in.
Let this world love, love less as I, love, love more,
even if it leaves me to only love myself.

Love, love more

For us to get free, not enough love.
Too much blood running round me.
Too many mad ways, killing us dead.
Can't take a second to hear a bird fly.
Sitting alone in a park, on a bench, only able to cry,
Love, love more.
What can't we see?
Are we scared and prefer madness rather
than being life and free.
To soft for the hard grounds that lies under our feet.
Unable to change, unable to see.
Love, love more, crying forever more,
Praying the Lord hears our inner tears
And helps us find the door.
It really hurts daily, living without,
Knowing its wonder is what we're all about.
Stop and listen to that newborn's cry and without fail,
You will know the reason why.
Love, love more, forever help us fly.
Knowing without this gift, we all would die.
We only have to remember just what your
Mother's Mother's mother said to you and have faith in all
your actions and all the things you do.
Hear my voice, if only for three words
And love, love more and fly like a bird.
Stop the madness. Don't call it life.
There's stronger than that and you should definitely
think twice.
Let's take care of all.
Make it better and well.
Let's love, love more,
Let's ring the bells.

*Let everyone know this better way.
Let's all love, love more, from your heart today.*

Flowerbed

How red a rose, thorns sprouting
Outward love. The reds shinning
Over the black, lighting a way to
A place not found, thought forgotten
And thought of no more.
We will tend to ourselves alone
And let man have his rule.
Let man praise without love.
Let them walk into a desert of illusions.
They say they can live without the rose.
They say they don't have to cry.
So let them have theirs and I will hide
In my bed of roses forever.

4those that love

For those that love,
seeing what you're doing to hurt that other,
is the first step for better but,
if that step is not seen or ignored,
and the pain continues flow,
the love can't remain or
could have ever been so strong.

Why do we have to fight for love?

Only Dreams

And now there are only the dreams we hold onto.
Hopes that they only come true.
Ready to only offer what we have, in trust that our
gift is kept safe and cared for through time.
No hard words or selfish ways creeping into each
own space but thanks and appreciation for the gift
given to us both.
I know that in my birth I was given the gift of love,
bestowed upon me from angels that made the word.
I feel it running through my vein while I breathe and
understand its power.
To you my love, I openly give it all without care,
To you.
I pray it is understood and wanted by you for the
angels that gave it to me, has lead me to you and
My gift is yours forever.

Eggs in the snow

Eggs in the snow,
In the middle of July,
Basking on their side
Without rolling over.
Eggs in the snow.
Only revealing its purity in its yolk.
Still basking but rolling over the Snowman's feet.
Rolling as a sled might roll
As it tumbles downhill,
Over the snowman's feet.

Eggs in the snow

Music is

Music is the only path we follow.
We hear no song from less
And refuse to live without.
Kill my body but never able
To take my sound.
Till the end it shall be
And I will breathe no other air.
Music will be mine
For I am hers forever.

So hard

I can remember the way you smelled
As I drowned in love with thee.
Being lifted above the clouds to clear spring
Skies of turtles going slow because they just
Walk that way and to dolphins leaping higher
Than high to kiss and fall free to a body of endless
water and dreams.
Where is that something that's missed so dear.
How could I have misplaced it?
My words are frozen in time with myself.
I'm standing here at the station praying she
Comes to pick me up.
I'm sad because I know the truth and it comes
Back to myself, the truth of my own now.
My brother said, "it's because I have not addressed
My yesterday and I think everyone is stupid because
they don't understand".
Well, maybe it's all true and I don't even know it.
I just wanted to smell something nice for once
And love more than I was shown.
I just never thought it would be so hard.

Food and Water

Love is the food and water for the life.
It keeps us still as our planet spins round its axis and it keeps us from falling off into a world less natural.
A world of demands without reason and acts
Without care.
Love is life, so live it till death...

Mistakes

*Wanted to hear the noise over the noise In my mind.
Wanted to go out and try to remind myself of
My worth and my beginnings.
Seeing myself through eyes of young.
Seeing myself make mistakes as I wait for love.
I can hear my friends speaking the truth to me.
Advising me and reminding me.
Me of all to forget and get
Caught up in all the madness.
Playing tug of war with my heart and mind
As I watch from childhood eyes at myself
Falling into the state of an old man with leather hands.
Trying to guide all the children as they play.
Telling the world all the words
I never was able to hold.
Warning them to watch themselves and their brothers
for danger lurks out of everyone's door and when its
mist fills your lungs, mind and heart, you are able to
see the black angel above.
Beautiful and real,
Wishing you merely to climb into its arms
And be forgiven and blessed for your own struggles,
struggles that were a little more than,
Little house on the prairie.
Understood differently,
Maybe from city boundaries or age.
Maybe just from bad habits.
Where it comes from does not matter for as a man,
It does not matter what I had to carry.
All that matters is that you carry it to the end.
Feed your babies!
Pick up your chin!*

Be strong and know your worth!
Stop crying, it will be alright.
You know it's hard but, you have to be strong.
I know we're tired of where we are
And now is time to see.
Change your ways and be ready.
Sorry Charlie but, the dream is over.
Like you say, "Welcome to the NFL"!
I wonder how you could of
Forgotten where you come from?
Regardless of this or that,
There is still where you are
And what you do with it.
What we want different is within ourselves.
It's so easy to become so blinded.
See nothing but money or love.
It's so wicked how we so easily make mistakes.
Mistakes that are even
Questioned if they were mistakes?
Now, forget all cold hearts
And live with love in yours.
Be careful to remember to cry when it hurts.
It reminds you that your efforts,
However great or small,
Meant something in your heart.
Don't be your own fool for you can hurt you.

Butterfly

Butterfly
m butter-fly; 2n dash;
singen: warbble, butter-
fly kisses.

6

Thanks for u

You are a beautiful bird of multi-colors,
With wings that spread wide across the land,
Showering the hearts of children with gifts of
Motherlove and warm breast, were they may lay
Their heads and finally sleep after a long life's work.
You're that strength that will forever
Help us go on another day,
With truth, tears, and love,
All will be with help from you
And your gifts.

Thank you for being U

Fallen Angels

The sun was shinning bright the day I meet this
Angel see. I did not know at the time that she was
The one to release me.
As she walked among the masses, standing out some
what different than the rest. Humble and peaceful
with flowers upon her dress.
I was scared to speak for I did not know her name
but, something inside made me feel her clean,
Like the rain.
So I told her of tragedies pushed upon me in the
name of love and I think she understood as she
Smiled like a white dove.
In her eyes I could see for some time she was sad too,
for the love pulled her wings and left her a little
unsure too.
She said I could see her again, that she would take a
look at my world and for a moment I thought, maybe
this angel could be my girl.
Oh, what a joy to laugh together as time flew away.
I can't remember when another so, has made me
This happy.
The sun was shinning bright that day she let me hold
her hand and before I knew it, I wanted to hold her
again and again and again.
So now my head spins when I think of her soul, for I
see she is truly special, a wonderful friend to hold.
Just this past Sunday, she let me see her again.
We laughed and walked, she even let me hold
Her hand.
As the ocean breeze blew our wings about,
Something touched us see, something moved us about.

*It was something very special, no you could
Never miss. You see, it was these two angels blown
together to partake in their first kiss.
The entire world stopped to look and see what
Would happen next. Will these two angels fly free
Or be scared cause of the rest.
One flew away to the comfort of their home while
The other wrote it down, he even put it into a song.
Wondering if it's all just a dream or a fallen
Angel's game. Well if they never kiss again, there
Will be none to ever blame.
For the truth is that these two only want to
Fly, to be peaceful, loving and not a shame.
Never making the other cry.
Regardless I think it's true, for these two angels
Till the end, that no matter what tomorrow brings,
They will always remain as loving, true friends.*

Next Time

Soft wind brushing along my cheek.
A butterfly that passes,
Reminding you that today is your lucky day.
Watching young lovers from afar
As they question their own next move.
Hearing my son's laugh,
When he watches a funny on the tube.
Waiting patiently for the dog I was
Promised in my own youth.
Waiting on the next rain,
Just to catch a few drops upon my tongue.
Hearing the echo from friend's drinking,
Or just noticing a flower walk by.
And there's Mommy,
Always ready with another, "God Bless You"
And hearing my daughter talk a
Million miles a second, as she controls the situation.
I truly do get seasick but I truly love water as well,
So swimming in the life is similar in a way.
Loving the life but still feeling sick
From what's upon it.
I'm not talking about the butterflies or dragonflies,
I'm talking about us Man.
So simple, to live a life.
I live and practice daily life free.
It's not so far away.
Understanding the lines that were made
To keep us from crossing but, still seeing clear,
Which path is yours.
Trouble waters may be sailor's dreams
And children's laughter,
Could be a x-mother's nightmare.

To each is own...
But all have something upon our earth
Worth living for and should partake daily.
While we wish all well,
We must clean, mend and watch ourselves.
Sharing with open heart and humble minds,
Nothing more, nothing less...
See, I think this game of life is one that
Contains all elements and can be really fine,
As long as everyone follows the rules.

Lost and Found

Here is the love we lost before air was
Passed into our body. Our testament
Written that took us our own way,
Away from each other to learn and ready
Ourselves for each other.
Unborn dreams left from the fairy dust as
They flew over us in sleep.
Sleeping under a cloud unable to even
Remember the time we said,
"I'll see you and wait with the same love
I leave on your lips now".

Ripe Fruit

Will there ever be heaven for us?
The Promise Land laid with ripe fruit,
Falling from the vine.
Surrounded with hummingbirds and butterflies.
Soft wind blowing fairies about
And streams flowing with dreams of
Love and children.
Oh Lord; let me see the heaven with
Wisdom in my eyes.
Allow the tears to flow with overwhelming
Glee for happiness to be able to breathe its sweet air.
Sharing my greatest gift,
Love, love more.
Always giving a head start before I
Chase you round the apple tree.
One thought, to steal a kiss.
Oh, how sweet heaven must be and
I pray she will always be there for me.

You can't see music but you sure can feel it!

Kiss me

I don't even have to close my eyes
To dream and see you there.
As I sit here in this office,
My visions of you is too clear
And I wish to have you near.
Wonderful, wonderful lady
I have found and you move me beyond.
Kiss me again and again as our skin
Collides into abyss.

Kiss me…

Smile

Let's all take a moment to smile.
Regardless of the present moment we may be
faced with.
Regardless of the life knocking on our door.
Regardless of what we may have to live with.
Over money,
Over death,
Over man's bills,
Over our stress.
Above the job,
Above our children's future,
Above our wounds, it's just a test.
In us all lies a flower of light and warm days
To spread all around.
In memory with birth, a gift given with life,
We have to listen to our own sound.
Although clouds grow thick, trying to hide this
Simple beautiful fact.
It's still there in our hearts and my friends
We have to know that this is a fact.
So, why not?
It's free, guaranteed to make you feel good,
Just a simple smile from your heart to yourself,
So you can remember to fly free as you know
you should.
So smile,
So smile and let
The warm wind warms you all day.
So smile and take this with you,
As you go on your own way.

Smile.

Had a Wife

Use to have a wife.
She was right here you see.
She use to kiss me goodnight,
We use to be happy.
We did all kinds of things,
Always with passion you see
But, now my beautiful wife
Has gone away from me.
Sometimes I act like I don't care.
Full steam ahead on my way.
Other times I look round to see,
If my wife's still next to me.
Guess today's one of those days
When it's sort of hard to see.
Find myself thinking of my wife,
The only one for me, you see.
So we learn as we go,
Wishing sometimes we just know
And we don't have to lose our wives,
For us to know because we still must grow.
I guess I can only wish,
My wife is happy you see,
For she is a special lady,
Even if she's not with me.

Tender maps

Professor of good spirit.
Of strength besides courage
Along with her open heart
And open door to all.
Only wishing the best for all man.
Trying to bring families together,
Food to those that are hungry
Or education to those younger,
Letting them know that the world is
Truly theirs to make in whichever way they choose.
That all is well for the road will forever be fine when
Thy footsteps are upon soft ways and tender maps.
Just use your common sense
And use your ears more than your mouth.
Your own heart speaks.

Desert Flower

My desert flower, can you see her there?
Beyond the dunes, dressed in black with
Ruby red sapphires round her neck and hair.
She's dancing like a bird on a warm breeze,
Soaring cross our heaven sky.
So beautiful when I held her, she made me cry.
My desert flower, can you see her there?
Oh, how beautiful she is,
Glowing like the morning sun,
Leaving flowers along the path she danced over.
She dances without a care,
Without thought for herself she dances
Like love was meant to be,
With the force of thunder crashing into the sea.
No one can see her, no one but me.
My desert flower, can you see her there?
Hypnotizing my soul to long for her in my arms.
So near to kiss her hand and her call me her man.
This desert flower dancing for herself
And letting me see,
That this desert flower
Was truly meant for me.
Dance for me forever and let our love flow.
Try not to be scared,
For I'm scared too, you know.
The life is strange, the good and the bad.
If this was just a dream, I will go to my grave sad.
For this desert flower I see blooms year round.
My desert flower is the only music with sound.
So dance, dance, dance, then dance some more
And I will watch forever as my heart soar.
For life's message is love and this is all I hear,
As my desert flower dances and I hold her near.

Another Step

Gonna fly to see a friend.
Wondering if it's real or sin.
Another step forward,
Taking chances on notes we lost.
Trying to remember that loves the boss.
Sometimes blinded,
Overtaken by loud voices from the streets,
Reminding us that the price is high to pay if we lose.
Remembering the pain and still seeing the bruise.
Too lost to cry in the presence of friends
Because of their laughter,
Thinking it's a joke
And love's a game that ends.
So which note will I play
And will it be heard
Or will life only offer
What man thinks we deserve,
And who is that man
That laid down that law,
And if he was a good man,
How could he let love fall?
Why am I going to see this one I call friend,
And when I get there
Will they love me till the end?

Much More

There must be more love than my eyes see.
All these man's child, so bitter from holding back
Tears that were made to fall.
Monkeys on backs and chips on shoulders.
Reckless from giving up on their plans of greatness.
Angry because their mothers went to their graves
penniless after working a hard life through.
Lost in the world, rather a part of her sister sun.
I say there must be more love than my eyes see.
Love to cut through all this sickness
And disease I speak of.
Just as many have suffered and many have prevailed.
Some out of luck but many out of determination in
Their pursuit to make their dreams possible and bear
The stone, cast at them many times before.
Pain hurts and death offers you no time but,
Love is always there in each and every one
That has passed out of their mother's womb.
I know there is more love out there and I pray we
All remember soon so that we can live as close to
Heaven while on earth, as we can.

Well, who

Who's to say when you understand
And see the sand pass through the glass
And the time slip away.
To say goodbye to all those wonderful
Things you held so dear and close to one's
Own heart and mind.
So what, if no one was able to understand
You on your journey into the next day.
You're still standing and tomorrow will still come.
If it just a dream, then thy should die with it gripped
To one's own forgiveness and promise.
It's o.k. not to let go of the gold
That's too heavy to carry alone.
Just think, tomorrow there may come a child
To help one remember that the
Weight is not so great.
It's more the way you carry it.

Love is Like Trees

Seems like love is like trees.
Real bright in the summer.
Little cloudy in fall.
Bear in the winter and eager in spring.
In Hawaii the sun always shines and
The flowers are always sweet.
In the mixed up Mainland, it's very
Easy to break down and cry about it all.
Never can say if I'm on tomorrow's love list.
One thing I can't really say for sure.
Have tried.
Sometimes I feel like I'm doing real good.
Then there's other times when it seems
Like the sun will never shine.
I do get up!
I do believe!
Sometimes I must say, it's hard and I
Just want to leave it for the next butterfly but,
That's not fair. So, what's a man supposed to do?
I don't know.
There's a reason for all that we go over in life,
All that we see.
If you truly do learn from your lessons and
Practice real hard what you've learned,
Then maybe, just maybe,
You can become one of the lucky ones.

Maybe?

Bullets

Bullets
f bullet; math.,geogr. sphere;
sp. shot; spherical killer,
ballbearings(s pl)

7

Innocent children

This is killing me.
Tearing me limb from limb.
I can't cry now for I am around strangers
That could never understand this pain so deep.
The tight grip upon my heart that's bleeding my
Love dry. The grip of soft hands that do not let go.
Left numb from the test that has broken dreams
And melted love to tears that burn like wax,
Rolling down my cheek.
How I need a hug at this moment by my love.
To rest my head upon her breast and rest.
To finally sleep and dream again, is what's needed for
this solider.
The war has went on far too long and should have
never been fought.
Senseless Murder, innocent children of God lying on
their backs, pleading for mercy, for help.
CAN YOU HEAR ME?
Has it become easier to pull your trigger?
Are you setting yourself up to shoot me between
The eyes with more surprises?
Can't you see the white flag?
How long must I wave it before you stop shooting?
Please stop this senseless killing, for I want to go
home and sleep.

My Prison

So I bring this pen to pad after many walks,
Many tears, many days.
Awakening to the loud sounds outside my door.
Eyes opening, seeing the prison I locked myself in.
Not understanding that another prison has been
built around the first one.
Not knowing even in my own home, mine eyes
Were closed.
Understanding not, what was smiling in my face
But flying away daily.
Deceived by honor and the role I played in being this
good man and how could I have known these types
Of people, liars and thieves, stealing my goodness as
they played house with my child and me allowing
their poison vines to wrap around my throat and pin
Me to the wheel.
Standing around pointing their fingers as they hide
their madness behind faces of etiquette, position and
the foolish notion that they are the best.
Sad but now mine eyes are open and I have opened
the door of this prison I built and knocked down the
Prison made by others.
Unclear to them today but, engulfing them tomorrow,
As I rebuild my castle as I have been taught years
before they knew.
Tomorrow is almost here and I shall be ready.

No

Started to open my eyes to see
Why yesterday was so hard.
Seeing all the madness and unnecessary
Ways of those that called me friend,
Threw rocks at me and called up noise.
People that think they know so much,
While locked behind doors of fear.
Liars, trying to speak of love.
I'm going to the store. I'll be right back.
Liars having their way
With the good in me.
To think I let their way shadow my own,
Is something I will learn never to allow again.
To be knocked down, begging for someone to
Care and told to believe that the only way was
To lie and read yourself.
To understand that war and blood
Were the only ways to settle it all.
No!
There are other ways,
Easier roads that are not from hurting ones dear
Or for hurting us.
I will never understand how people can make such
decisions that hurt others so but I will offer a prayer
in hopes that time will change us all.

Some Lie

So where have all the birds flown?
Why is it so dark and cold today?
I can't hear any children playing
And there are no stars in the sky?
Where has all the love in man gone and
Why do some lie?
Why ask my name, if you want not to know?
Tossed about on a sea of tears,
Adrift without food or water.
Just left to die.
I'd rather be marooned on an island,
Left all alone, then kiss one that loves me not
To the bone.
So by myself, me and I,
I guess I must wait till real love shows her
Wonderful colors but till then,
Mine heart, shall slowly die.

Monsters

*Sometimes you do think there are monsters out there
And you become that child that needed the closet door
Closed and the light left on enough to make a break
for the door when he shows himself.
Sometimes you're really scared of just things and you
Need to be held, to feel safe.
To feel the warmth, comfort, safety and love
from one you hold dear. Just that simple sign of
affection, can be enough to run all the monsters back
into their hole in the closet, and sealed away forever.*

No more monsters!

No Dicks

Life is the biggest thing around and
It's full of wonderful and awful things.
It's easy and it's hard.
It's mostly what we make of it.
If you want sun,
Then have it.
If you want rain,
Then swim in it.
If you want to be a loving, warm soul,
Then express this and it should return ten folds over.

If you want to be a d—k,
Wait around, someone will come sooner or later and
F—K YOU!

I guess this big world can be a much nicer place
If the people in it, decided to just be nicer.

Signed,
NO D—KS ALLOWED!

Love, right?

So what's up?
Are you strong now?
Did you let love, let go
To the next phase of life?
Brushing yesterday under
The carpet as you look in
Another's eyes and say,
"I love you". So hard when
Here but, so easy to go on
The same trail that lead us
To our end.
Want me to be happy
Or find happiness, is what you say.
You, so strong, to be able to go
Forward without thinking about
The words that you convinced me of.
Those words that I believed
In and cherished.
So what if you're gone?
I don't understand but, I can't
Spear energy to care because it's
Only love anyway, right?

*The meaning of any
kind of Love,
Is to always care.*

Who's True

How can we tell if one's words are true?
Because of chastisement that comes in
The form of buildings falling on top of
You in the form of harsh words and stern fist.
How can one tell?
I say I can't but, I can believe in God to show
Me my way. I can be as true as the wind shall blow
Regardless of those men that smear the meaning
Of truth, love, honesty and will.
Regardless of the lies our world may tell.
I can only understand that there's no rulebook
For anyone to follow. There is the spoken word
Of the Bible and its words are of the purest nature.
Even hard to follow those rules,
For we are all sinners. The questions that forever
ponder my mind till that 3 o'clock hour when the
tears blind the light in our own soul.
The answers must be inside,
Eating at the gut and mind.
Your own understanding from all the shots that
Echoed through the hall telling you
To duck or die.
My say's, I have not failed me.
My question is, have I just not understood the signs?

Cars

Tried to give my air to a dying man today.
Pushing my life into him with prayer.
Hearing the blood run into our street
From cars too fast that were not supposed to meet.
I failed!
My air was too weak and this man he died.
Simply went to sleep.
You see right away the color blue take over.
Not knowing his name, just that my air was
Not enough.
Was it this or did he want life no more.
It all went black and the music playing was screams.
And what about me?
How could I be spared?
Who said I could walk away?
Why was I spared?
Because I love,
Because children or kin?
Am I unique because I have a friend?
Why is the life so little till we think were big?
I do not know but, still a grave they will dig,
4him

My skin

And how can a father teach thy child so
Young to hate me because of my blackness?
Am I less than the next because of this fact?
Can they not see my beauty shine beyond my skin?
Can't my love out way yesterday's ignorance?
Why would that child even open thy ears to such
noise and act against me unconscious or not,
Allowing those ideals to sip into those actions
Toward my goodness?
The one that was suppose to be loved,
Treat me less than I am.
Throwing lies and hard words my way,
Thinking it fair and I deserve no less
Than what thy father has offered.
So blind they cannot ever come close to
understanding that I should be treated no less
Than the king my mother bore.
It is not O.K.!
Anyone can proclaim love, with understanding this
Is a crime against all my ancestors and those that act
in this fashion,
Never deserve my time or love.
Sad to know that I cannot produce enough love and
sunshine to make those that cast their rocks at my
glass heart to merely stop and act toward me as
They wish others acted to them or to their own
mothers long ago.
I guess it's not in my control.
I cannot concern myself with this noise,
for it only confuses my own and makes me small
from trying to prove something that God
Already confirmed.
May God bless them and be their judge.

Mercy

So how do we keep this monster caged?
Taking punch after punch, giving only a flinch.
Wishing for mercy from complete strangers that
Proclaimed their un-dying friendship
On far away lands.
Dr. King vs. Malcom X.,
All these that stand by and watch,
Know too clear how wrong it is.
Stuck in their tracks, paralyzed, unable to make
Any move without a leader to lead.
A lot of followers, following the wrong way.
I guess my bars that hold me are made with truth
Within the reality and love for all mankind,
Knowing only its sickness at the end of that road.
So I withhold my feelings for brighter times to come.

No smell

And now I look upon scorn faces.
No emotions streaming outward.
No smell in the kitchen to remind
One of a good meal at one time or another
And to think of children running a mock
Through their streets, is unheard of
And the only light on is within my own window.
No music in thy streets and no dance of true
Romance besides that on one of the four
Programs they show on their television.
A bunch of Benz's, build stiff and steal to
Withstand all types of conditions.
Never feeling a thing.
Only knowing that they have to
Get to the next station.

Here I Am

Here I am, beat'in and tired.
Holding onto tomorrow's promises
Of golden pots and candy yams.
Looking from the inside in,
To another real of sunshine I carry on my brow.
Who's to say tomorrow will come
And grant me the pleasure of breath.
Who can say?
The law,
The way one man's
To walk to the next.
The getto they say,
The hood of my bread'ren,
Were my sister so young took
That shot to the head.
Where mommy opened her legs
For Mr. Goodbars and my brother
Did time because of his name.
Who's to say what they think I'm about
For I live in France, Nice is nice you see.
Eating dog in Hawaii cause it's the local way.
Would they even be able to understand,
Thinking I don't know my way.

No excuse

Back to these streets,
full of the sorest faces I've seen in the planet.
Such caught up hate and 1940 behavior,
One's only wish is to say, "I am of a better man.
I can build it higher and touch the stars before
Any man and look back down upon the other
man and say, "No good" or "other color Oustlander,
need leave our land and go back
to where they were raised,
upon thy streets of anger and pain".
Do I lift a hand out of anger or
must I protect my own soul?
My own manhood.
My own child.
So much sickness from my own brother human.
So much ignorance from those that think they
know better or can merely out match.
Upset at the world but, throwing sticks
at the wrong man just because they're near.
Is that a reason?
Can I excuse that other man because yes,
I understand just how hard the life is
or must I excuse not,
for I must bear the
Same hard street.

No excuse

Agony

Agony in the dark over untouched food
And curious wonderings.
Reaching out to empty hands and non-given love.
Torture the mind with that carrot dangling in front.
Pushing forward and forward with thoughts
Of a reward at the end, for your sweat and pain.
Still climbing and scratching,
Trying to get to the top of closed doors.
Still holding onto things the masses gave up
On long ago.
Why do you try so? Take those licks.
Is it not clear the end holds not the love
You imagined anymore.
Have you just became so wrapped in the game
You've lost sight of the prize and reason.
Can't you see all of those gifts are gone?
All that's left I fear are dirty socks
And mothball eaten shirts.
No more cherry vanilla kisses of joy.
You keep playing a game that has already been lost.
You're a knight on a quest for love lost
In a thorny rose garden that will leave
Your hands blooded and torn.
Your quest of love, love more is over and done.
Go now, be clear
And save your love for the sun.

Stars

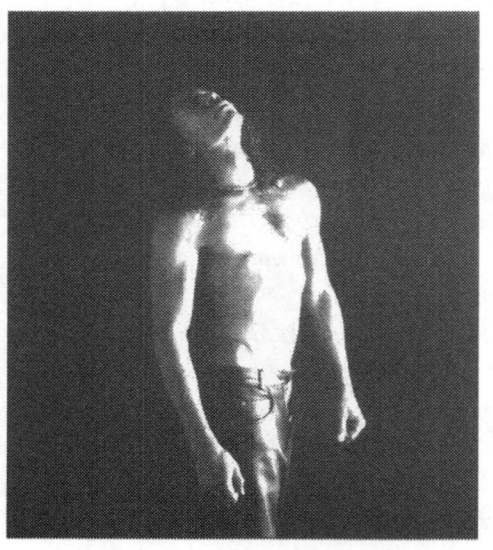

*Stars
m star (a fig.) starry sky,
starkut, constellation,
shooting star; jewel*

8

Sun Break

Ever so often the sun may take
A break from its daily shine.
These times may seem so bleak
And sorrowful that one can easily
Forget what it ever felt like to be warm.

In these times, although it may be hard,
We have to look behind all the darkness
And find what is just resting dormant.
We have to know beyond a doubt that that
Warmth of our sunshine has not abandoned us.
That it's just resting and will
Return sooner than we expect.

You see flowers cannot grow if
There is only sunshine to live on.

It needs cold air, dark nights and wet days.
It all is a part of the big plan, that plan that
Leads to wonderful, wonderful things
And makes so many happy,
In the form of a flower.

So know where your sunshine is
And know it's right there with you.

There's life

This world so big and full of different sweets,
Different flowers and colorful fishes.
There is sunsets on warm days and
Lovesexy moons close enough to touch.
There is children's laughter
In the streets as they play
And lovers deafening each other's
Air as they passionately kiss.
There are lakes still and peaceful,
And snow to melt and full.
There are dogs and music
And trees to help us breathe.
There are fathers and mothers
Those wipe the fears from our cheeks
And there is God for strength
We find in ourselves.
There's the birth of a new born
To say there can be a better tomorrow
And there is love.

Our Mother's Child

Don't think.
Don't try to move the world.
Just let it be.
It seems like we have the power to make it happen.
In fact, we know our power is great enough to move
mountains, just because this is so.
We may not see it happening as it is but,
This does not mean, it is not.
Remember that you are the most beautiful child
In this world and you are great.
God has not forgotten, nor has he left your side.
It just may not be as clear as we like.
Believe that it does exist.
You're the one, that star shinning over head,
Brightening the trail that leads to greatness.
With time, pain in learning and love in heart,
It will all become clear.
So, I guess that we must stay strong,
Hold on and not forget that we are our
Mother's children and in the end this is good.

Did anyone notice?
Birds fly...

A star

Stars that blink and twinkle off one's eye.
Far, far away. Try to catch one if you can fly.
Star bright, shinning over us all.
Help some to believe instead of tears that fall.
They say when you're great, you are given this name.
As a singer, an actor, anyone that finds fame.
Such an appropriate word, if you're chosen to be one.
A star to help us smile or cry depending on what
you've done.
Sitting up high in the heavens, so close around
The moon. Scared if they fall out the sky, one
Can bring us all doom.
I guess it's best they stay high and twinkle in the night.
Good for wishes, a thing that always makes
Us feel right.

Oneself

So we're born upon this earth naked, alone.
Raised on a block, a community,
Our neighborhood.
Then most remain for the familiar taste of
Food or for friends from grade school.
Scared to leave behind our childhood, our love.
Who's to say better here or there?
Isn't it what we make?
Because a star falls from the sky,
Can one say the moon will fall too?
Can we say our love will forget?
Scary stuff, chances to take or not chances at all,
Just belief in one's own.
Strength to carry on till the next day with glee.
I know I can.
I think I can,
Is what the little train said rolling up that hill.
In heart and mind is where all answers lye for oneself
And within ourselves, lye's the keys for all doors.

Her baby

You are something to see, when you're happy,
When you're sad, when you're just running free.

Not one can deny, after seeing you in the eye.
No words can explain and if some do,
They may make you cry.

Your mother must be happy to say,
That her baby has grown with love,
Making others happy.

All walks of man must clearly see,
That you're something special, like a
Kiss in spring.

Oh, how wonderful, this must all make you feel.
So please continue to live up to this fact and keep
It real.

What a shame if no one takes a thought to learn
more of what you do.
I'm sure their eyes may open and they too may learn
To be free too,

For you are truly something wonderful, wonderful
To see.
Thank you Mommy for saying these things to me.

Thanks Mommy

Water

Here's another early morning.
I can feel the birds in the trees
Un-nestling to the smell of dew on the leaf's tops.
Through this, I ponder over yesterday,
Now and tomorrow,
Wondering if my steps have lead me
In the wrong direction,
If it all is just an illusion?
Something made up all of the dreams I carried alone.
Could I be so blind and confused in
The name of love?
To see an oasis in a desert and gulp sand!
Believing in all the days and moons that's
Passed as I tried to reach it.
Knowing it would quench my thirst.
Knowing it was there.
Now as I sit with this sand in my mouth,
I begin to see that I must have been going
In the wrong direction all along.
As I see the truth in my steps,
I know that I was real,
Standing for what I have been true for.
I sadly feel that help and effort did not play apart.
I feel shame for working alone as master cracked
their whip across my back and changed my name,
Telling me to change as they cared none for
Their own.
Only acceptance for what hurt they do.
An illusion I see.
Something you think is there.
You swear you see it.
You even told each other it was there.

And it could be found for ourselves,
But to sit here with this sand in my mouth,
I know it all was just an illusion.
May I find water soon.

Start today

Tied up in knots over the day.
Unclear roads ahead,
Looking for the right way.

Who has the answers?
Any words for me?

A path leading to lands full
Of love and harmony.

We know that it is hard
But we must not give up.

We can make it, turn it right,
In life there's more
than just showing up.

We can be the better man.
We can do it, we know the way.

Lend a hand,
Be a better man,
Come all,
Please start today.

Wonderful day

Today's to be a wonderful day.
The flowers are suppose to open
Their hearts and share the wonderful
Scents that God has blessed them with.
The sun and rain are suppose to spray together
Into a rainbow of colors so brilliant,
All are left blinded with enough gold
In their hearts so at the end,
They can only smile with glee.
The birds are set to fly to the heavens
With their soft song trailing and falling
Into the ears of hearts unturned,
Filling and strengthening all
That their beliefs are true.
Help them understand the powers
Are on loves side.
Today the children are supposed to play hopscotch,
Tag with notes and sing a song special for the day.
Today is supposed to be a day made anew.
No other in my way and not even you.
I guess this day without love,
Is no better than the rest.
Just dreams and dreams
And dreams like the rest.
Just for it to be true,
Without this or that.
Without nothing more than it to be true.
How else can we hear the birds
When they sing in their flight
And the children's laughter,
Even with their fights.
What about the rainbows,

What gold can it bring?
As all the flowers scents
Fade so far away from me.

Hold On

What's going on man?
What in the hell are you doing?
Ignoring signs again?
Being ignorant for love!
Where really in your heart,
Do you think you stand in their eyes?
Do you really think all your love
Is recognizable to tell?
You're setting yourself up for failure and pain,
For the signs say that you are already forgotten
And your mind and heart are just playing tricks on
you because you want there to be real water at the
oasis in your eyes.
The signs have it,
So now understand and grow.
Wish nothing but heaven for the one you love in soul.
Cry when needed but always hold on.

2love

Us

Us, is a word that fills my eyes with tears,
My heart with passion, and my mind
with dreams of forever.
To let one's imagination flow freely
Across all around, only seeing that which
You believe in and holding it near as a baby
Cooing in his mother's warm pouch,
Protected from the dangers around but,
Free to roam the land and explore its many wonders.
Us, is all of my three wishes wrapped into one,
And I pray this wish of us is true.

Child's Giggle

There are times when you look out that window
From your own mind, to see flowers and rain.
Those children's faces that make you sort of
Giggle to yourself, and you begin to feel that
It's really worth.

These are the times you must hold dear,
For tomorrow can bring those clouds that seem
To shadow over the colorful ideals we carry
In ourselves.

Hiding the reminds of a child's giggle.

So remember.

I am me

I am me, man,
The wrong doer with the left hand.
I am this and that.
I am alive.

Getting Hard

Getting hard to breathe again.
Hard to catch my air.
Getting cloudy and dark,
Too cold to cry out, Please!
Not sure about tomorrow,
I Guess the pains still there.
Gets even harder to cry when
You think, who cares?
Rather be truthful and
Hold my head high.
Rather look my children in
The eyes, knowing never a lie.
Be still my heart, the
Blue skies on its way.
You will soon climb mountaintops,
Swim in seas and with your children,
Fly away.
Bide your time wisely,
Watch your step my friend so your
Light can shine for all in the end.
A prince on black stallion,
With platinum sword,
Riding into battle,
Never letting life be bored.
In the end your castle waits
For you, so be yourself
No matter what you do.

The Instrument

Your body is the instrument that releases
The music from the soul. Made with love
To be shared with all around the globe.
You have been chosen to lead our army.
Soldiers of music that are millions strong.
Chosen to fight the darkness in unsure people lost.
The gift given you contains messages in
Sound for those that need most can hear.
You can say a healer in a way with
Strength that can't be matched or duplicated.
What is only needed is your own
Understanding in the gift you behold.
You're mastering of your own sound
You're transmitting. With this realization from
Your own soul, comes a key to unlock that
Door that holds many wonders and gifts.
Listen closely to your soul and your heart
For they hold the answers to all for you
And wait for your usage of them.

Music is waiting for you
I hope you find it.

To Ash
Love, Dad

Adam

Another role I play.
Adam his name. The man of men.
All of man in one.
Sacrificing a rib to form women.
Temptation, a word used describing
The taste of a sweet apple which in
Truth was the awakening of mankind
And his down fall.
Strange to think of me being chosen by man,
Directed by God to play such a role.
I wonder if I am a walking spirit that
Walks past the others as a dream.
Transparent to those around,
Just a vision that people desires to
Look upon but too Holy to touch.
Am I alive because I breathe?
Am I alive because I exist?
If so, what is this strange air around I?
Why am I floating above myself,
Crying over the world,
Over love, over so much not connected
Directly to me in any way?
Why is this so strong in I
And could this have any connection
With this role Adam I play?
I can only wonder.

Me

Build it and they will come.
Thinking positive in the New Year.
Going forward and claiming that rainbow
That belongs to me.
Brushing off the dust so I'm clean again.
Wiping the sand from my eyes so I can see.
Standing tall, walking past danger with smiles of
sureness and truth in my tomorrows, for I am me
And this is good.

Me!

Don't Cry

Don't cry sweet lady over the
Blood spilled over my road.
The bruises have healed well over time.
The end of my road is nowhere near
And I still see clear rainbows smiles and
Clear blue days.
Although life can cast stones into our
Glasshouse, we need not break.
We are strong children that were once King.
We have not forgotten the words whispered
Into our ears before birth.
We remember that our meaning is not all laid
Out on a table at one time.
We remember that we must be patient and wait
To gain full understanding from all that life's offered,
We remember what was whispered in our ears
And we will wait without so many tears.
We remember

Sleepy

Another day has closed and this
Nightwalkers feet are sore.
My pillow calls my name even
If I know it to be hard.
I pray for sweet dreams of paradise lost.
Warm days, soft smiles and wet kisses
To help us grow.
Take a moment to cry over nothing at all
Or just laugh till we roll in the mud without control.
Who cares is a question we ask.
Who hears the cries of souls lost in
Dreams broken by time and failure.
Ask me my name and I may stutter
Because I forgot.
Ask me why and I may not answer.
Sometimes the simple questions,
Are the ones we want least to ask
And sometimes answers are the last thing
We wish to hear.

Mother's Arms

Take time to love
And love upon a star.
Skies of greens and blues.
Let yourself be swept away
By glorious ideals we shared as children.
Stop the noise in your head and walk
Across the stream that leads to yourself.
Come'eth from your mother's womb
Knowing nothing but air.
So quickly love followed with her arms around you,
Keeping you so so warm and safe.
Only enjoying life's milk,
Sending us into such sweet slumber that
I do not remember how sweet that slumber
Must have been.
Your mother's arms

Mother told me

Stuck, stupid, dumb and drinking.
Today is life, regardless if we are in a strange land,
We call home. Yes, we want to cry loud and hard.
Yes, we have fear and it hits our heart hard.
Mother's milk cannot comfort this pain.
No music in my ear, just voices from the pain.
Looking upon ocean blue can make us smile
And we do.
Tempted to just die cause we can see the masses
and their lies.
Talked to a soul that truly felt the same.
Wanting to escape the game and do it without shame.
Wonder if we'll make it.
I already know we can.
I can see the pain from living in this place with
lost man.
I vow to never give up my true way.
I only hope those around will say,
"There goes a true soul.
One true to his way".
One that was able to ignore what they say.
For when the life is done, I only have God
and children to answer too.
When my soul lifts away, I have to answer anew.
A new path I made from the message put in me.
A new place for all man, all man to run free.
So what if I die. It was well worth the ride.
I will face it with head high. I will never hide,
for there is nothing more than the truth born
in your soul,
No more than this and it's something to hold.

Love, love more,
will forever be and I will always know this,
It's what my mother told me.

Close Your Eyes

Close your eyes my sweet.
Lay back in your mother's arms.
Feel the warmth of the day and the stars above.
Remember the sweet nothing in your ear,
As the clouds roll by.
Embrace the life and its wonders will prevail.
You are a special child of God,
And he will light away for you and I.
So hold your head high and fly on the wings of love,
Peace, rainbows and butterfly kisses,
With love as your guide to forever.

Lovers

Lovers
['lovers] 1. mates, partners;
friends, going steady;
2. explorers, support

9

So What

So what if she wants me not.
If she cannot see the truth of
My soul and my goodness.
So what.
We can't have all we want to have.
Actually, we can consider ourselves
Lucky to have all we do have.
I must say it's heavy on the heart
At times and I could not say why,
Things like this just make me cry
But, It does.

Romeo & Juliet

So milky soft her skin I touched. Stirring up
Reminds of forever after in love. The gentle curls
inlayed on top her head, black as the midnight sky.
Her legs entwined around and over mine as we sleep
under love's blanket wanting never to wake.
The sweet wetness of her sex dripping into a
Small pond on the tip of my tongue, my hand
caressing the curves along her waist, her hips,
her legs.
So much love I carry for her.
Too much to stay yet too much to go.
Can God not hear my plea?
Is it true my child will never be born?
And what of this love so powerful, So dear?
Will it lift in a mist to the heavens for angels
To carry to ones that have none?
Will our love lost be passed on to a family that
Needs to know of love's great power.
Have we sacrificed God's greatest gift because of
Our own blindness and clumsy ways?
Have we broken to many rules and now paying
The heavy price with loneliness, tears and fear of
forever no more?
I know of Shakespeare's tragedy of love,
Romeo and Juliet and I truly can and have cried
From never knowing of a story with such innocents
and courage for love.
I truly thought there could never be another story
That came close to this until now.
Knowing as I sit here alone, away from your scent,
your touch, knowing all we have fought for.
How we won and how we lost.

*Knowing all these things and feeling these hard
Tears drip down my cheek.
I can say that our story of love is truly more
Tragic than Shakespeare's Romeo & Juliet just because
at least they got to be together in
the end, even in death.*

Hold my Hand

Hold my hand tight if you must as the passion
Passes between our lips.
Questions of possible or not, of truth or not,
Of rain or snow.
Butterflies do fly naturally as children naturally play.
No force can change what is to be and to be lucky
enough to find a soul that connects with yours,
Is a blessing most are unable to see, let alone
Feel and believe.
Take care of the wind, even if you can't see it
For we need it to breathe.
One must remember they can fly even if most
Around try to ground us.
If we walk slowly sometimes, you may be able to
catch the faint smell of flowers or even hear a
caterpillar crawling to the next leaf.
Simple but true so we should never overlook
The obvious.

Can't

Can't hear your voice.
Can't look in your eyes.
Can't smell your skin.
Can't kiss your lips.
Can't whisper love me nots in your ear.
Can't share the morning dew with you.
Can't breathe.
Can't eat.
Can't think of life without us.
Listen closely to my heart beat your name.
I scream it from the mountaintops with no shame.
If you hear me, please answer my call.
If you love me, never let me fall.
If you miss me say and I'm there.
If you love me, forever play in my hair.
I pray your heart is as true as I think and
you see me as your man.
"Forever", you say,
If this is true, be rest assured
That I will be a good man.

Missing u

Loves

If love was the greatest thing on earth,
Why is it that love is sharp as a knife
That stabs the heart, rather than soothes?
Why is it so easy for someone that proclaims love,
To ill-treat the one they proclaim it to?
To think that love gives you the right to hurt,
Disrespect, lie to or not care for!
Is not the way love walks.
The steps formed into clouds leading to heaven,
Disappearing from under your feet,
Falling to the solid ground because your love
Cares not enough, to hold out their hand to catch
Your fall as they say, " I love you ", turn cheek,
Roll eyes and laugh in another's arms,
Because your love has spoken their words of truth
That you can't stand, That you use against them,
To push the knife in deeper than the life has
already done.
Why care if tears roll down your lover's cheeks?
You love them right!
So why do you have to catch their fall too?
Why do you have to control your viciousness?
Your words of hate.
You love them and they need not know more.
Love is...treating your love, less than love is?
No! This is not the love that
flows from my fingertips,
And not the love I will ever believe in.
Let this world love,
Love less as I,
Love, love more,
Even if it leaves me to only love myself.

The Lucky Ones

I heard a story some time ago about two souls
Drawn together in the early days over 50 years ago.
Meeting and marrying.
Promises exchanged, giving forever to each other.
One man, one women, one love. At the story end,
they were called the lucky ones because their
promises they kept in one way or another.
They were still standing in the end together.
The question of how they survived the many
Ups and downs was asked.
How two separate souls could remain living as
One for a half a century?
How quit, give up or change, did not mislead them
away from the promises made long ago.
They replied, "everyday is different, bringing
different events and different situations.
We treat each element as they come and let go
Of the events of the past".
As they spoke, you could see how easy they made it.
You could see that they were truly different but
Very much the same.
He was himself as she was woman.
There was love and respect for the differences
Of each. There was also a connection, an aura
Of love in each one's heart.
You could see that each would be happy when the
other finally made it home from the day.
You could see that an invitation for lunch or a walk
was welcomed with a smile.
You could see the little things counted.
So this is what I heard about the lucky ones and what
We tried to make for ourselves.

*If we can understand maybe we can be lucky as well.
The love was never there, just me living in a world
made by another's way not of my own.
For this, I shoot myself but have learned never to
give love even if it hurts the one that needs it
unless it's real in your heart as well,
Otherwise you may miss the real love you
Were made for.*

Keep Us Warm

Big kisses on hot sunny days are nice and
To find love in a lifetime is truly special.
God bless, soulmate,
What a word!
May we be this one I believe in and if so,
May her glory shine soon, just because
Winter's coming,
And we need her to keep us warm.

Lastnight

And there can never be a river
That flows as strong as the one
I hold in my heart for you?
Understand me not, just love me.
Just love, love more and never
Say it matters not.
Tomorrow the sun will shine
Over our hearts as they do now.
My love will be missed but in soul, in love.
I'm just lying next to you now and smell
The flowers that I pray to smell again.
Take care of love and nurse it to sweet slumber.
Embrace your dreams, given them strength to fly.
Don't cry too long without me near to hold.
Our tears can turn into knives with no mercy,
Tearing our souls to shreds.
Let, I love you rule over us both.
Knowing space and time can never change this.
I was told, I have the power to make clouds
Disappear as I walk on water and swim in dirt
And if it's true, then I guess we all should be
Able to at least love as our souls know how.

Another space and time.

Beata

How can I express this moment while
My head spins round and round.
My heart pumping warm blood through my veins.
Each thump crying your name.
Feeling it full of love from the heavens.
Pinching myself to see if I truly am awake,
If this really is true.
Remembering my words
Of never again.
Remembering tears rolling down my cheek
As I forced myself to sleep,
Wishing for nothing but another day to end.
To believe so strongly in true love but,
Not tasting its fruits, is an awful way to live at all.
Forever holding onto a dream,
Wondering if only crazed ideals ruled me.
Seeing man walk over man,
Women over women, without a care for true love.
Brushing it into a pile of dirt and sweeping it
Under the carpet like it belonged there.
I remember seeing the door that said give up!
Love is a ghost that will only haunt me
And leave me petrified and in shock.
I almost went in that door of no turning back
But, somehow I turned, only telling all that
Love does exist,
That regardless of the clouds blown out by man,
It exists and is more powerful than any man,
Word or law.
I remember how it felt to wait for her whisper
In my ear, saying, " I'm home".
Love at first sight, catapulting us into a

*Different world. A world we both built apart from each other,
One block at a time. Building our own thoughts and desires
For ourselves. Knowing when the time came, when the love
we knew true, revealed itself, our block house would
Be complete with doors open, awaiting your coming.
Now you're here and I have never been so warmed
Knowing that I was right. Knowing you were there and would
Come as long as I believed.
Welcome my love.
Please make yourself comfortable for forever,
For that is what love is for me and in this man,
Rest a glass heart to share with one.
Let it be you, as I swear to all, you're my love forever,
For I have heard your call.*

Forever after

By My Own Hand

By my own hand,
I plucked the rose from its stem.
Although I meant no harm,
I committed a sin.

No matter how hard I tried,
And wished to hold her near,
The art took me away,
From the one, I held so dear.

It started at the top of the day,
We had so many plans,
We wanted to fly so free,
Into wonderful lands.

Then at the last minute,
The art, it took me.
So now I may never see her again,
What's left is the art and me.

I cry cause I think,
She thinks me like the rest,
Just some dude that wants to do her,
Just get in her dress.

This is not so,
There is truth within my way,
And now I guess only God will know,
That I just wanted her to be happy.

Roses are Red

Roses are red
And violets are blue.
From the bottom of my soul,
I'll always love you.

The years have passed and we've worked
Oh, too hard but, I know it's been worth,
Love is nothing to discard.

May you understand and feel,
Maybe you even lend a hand.
May you forever wish for love and
Have me as your man.

I do.

What I would do

I was just thinking what I would do
If I was walking down the beach,
With the sea brushing up my leg,
And I saw a few birds,
And a couple of rainbows.

What I would want to do at that time,
And I came up with the decision that
I would only wish to kiss you.

Just a thought

Sum water
Sum light
Sum love
Sum life...
Sum flowers...

I wish you Love

I wish you love and peace in your day.
I wanted to tell you that you are a wonderful flower
upon this crazy planet and your mother
Could be proud of the person you have grown to be.
Withstanding the storm and still standing with grace.
Lord knows how I was able to come upon you in my
lifetime and what it all means.
How I can even feel warm or cold again,
Is strange indeed.
No answers but many thanks that you have came.
I hope that you are able to see me for the man I am
and have good feelings when I come to mind.
I hold your hand now and kiss your lips later.
Sweet, sweet lady I have found.
May you always be true and know that you
Forever have a friend in me.

Talk to me

Talk to me my love.
Share kind words with me.
Try to forgive yesterday's
Madness and let's be.
Life, such a looking
Glass from front to back,
Foiling yesterday's dreams while
Leaving love to fend for itself.
Share kind words with me for
You know I love you.
Speak not of hate or of thoughts
That are more confusion than fact.
Free us sweetie and hear my
Heart beat with yours.
It never stopped
And never will.

Careless

As the time passes, we feel our heart tighten with
Rage from extending ourselves and love to you.
Although weak and sad, we still have the strength
To stand and see the wrong thrown in our direction
By you for oh, too long.
Regardless of upbringing or ideals formed,
We think you selfish and foul for being so careless
with our heart.
Care not of the broken glass you lay at our feet.
Go on with life and find whatever you think love is,
for we have a different dream that we can keep
For ourselves. Try not to understand, just go on with
your ideals and ways.
We're sure your hardness will help you believe
yourself and see us not again in your heart.

Xxxxx

I love her

There she lies,
The slumber blowing across her dreams...
So sweet, she sleeps,
My dream of love.

Will she ever know
How I love her dear?
Can she remember the time,
In my head so clear,

Or is it she's forgot,
How to wish me near?

There's a soul out there
Looking to love.
Talking about that love,
That's sacred from above.

As she sleeps with her purest glow,
I love her.
I love her that's all I know.

As bullets of fear and rage pass me by,
As I lie in my mess,
As I cry.

Lord!
Stop the noise!
Let me sleep once in a life.
I love her.
I love her. Please make her my wife.

How can I say more?
What more can love do?

Love's the power that leads us,
Please let it lead U.

There will never be more.
Maybe more, you will find,
Love is wishing the best,
Regardless, the crime.

If I was a penny today, oh, what will I do?
Be worth more than life'
All just because I love U.

Could it be U

Could it be u?
So close, could be blood.
Friend, sister, lover,
Stopping only to smell flowers,
Knowing time is short but
Hearts are dear.
Waking in the middle of the night
Reaching out to the sound of your
pumps going down the hall.
Wondering daily if I come to mind,
even in the smallest whisper.
Knowing the truth could never
Overpower destiny waiting....

Signed Flowers

Just left

Why do I miss you?
Just saw you a second ago.
Your eyes and rhythm,
Moving across the room.
Leaving a trail of flowers in bloom and you.
Do you see me there even though I'm gone?
Are you able to make the noise around come silent?
To be able to hear my heart?
Has man stripped you of trust in yourself,
Your ideals from childhood of love?
Can you believe?

Missed you

Missed you much today.
Wished hard to see you
But it didn't happen.
Not enough time in the day.
Maybe tomorrow or just
Later, who can say?
Am I just lost in an imaginary
World of fools looking to
Claim you all for my own?
Pouring out love me nots and
Promises of forever?
Is this even what you want
Or is it just in my head?
No one wants to be a fool for love,
Just in love.
I pray my years has taught me
And you're true, for if I miss you
In vain, I would know not what to do.
Well, sleep tight my love and think
Of me from the heart if I'm there.

Be still

If love must live as a fantasy, then let it be.
My soul lives for my soulmate even if I can't
See her, I know she will wait.
The test to determine if you can even be blessed
Is within the way walked and if you will settle
For less, if you give into temptation because you
Just want to hit it like the rest.
Be still and listen.
You may be able to hear your soulmate that waits
For you.
Try and feel it there.
No it's not easy to just sit and wait.
Believing that in time, you will see your soulmate.
If you give up my friend, you'll be lost forever
And the reward you long for will turn into
Never more.

Be still and listen.
In your heart you will find and if you're good,
In your soul, your soulmate you will find.

So believe and have faith.
She won't let you down.

Spank Me

Please spank me.
I have been a bad boy.
I have eaten all the cookies
In the jar and yes,
I want more!
Lock me in the closet
And only see me on Sunday
After that fine meal.
Just don't forget I'm down there
And come one day and forgive.

Sex

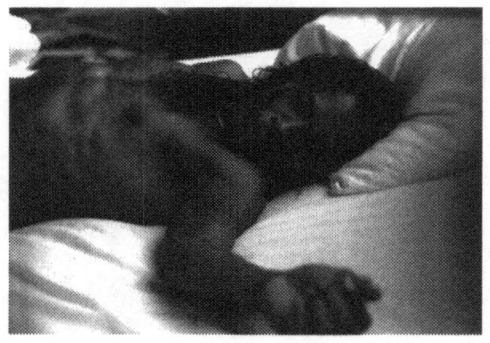

Sex
['sex] kind, species;
Familie: family; gender
sexual: inter-course

10

For I miss

For I miss thy scent
And thy touch across mine chest.
Or is it just my fantasy,
Or is it just the wind?

Bad Thing

Could it ever be a bad thing?
To wish to make love to such
A beautiful flower as yourself?
To willingly offer my sex in
Exchange for yours?
Real passion melting into night,
feeling me fill your cup and taste your all.
Could this ever be bad for
I cannot resist your pheromones
Floating up and out of you,
Clearly giving yourself away,
Letting me know that you wish
Me inside of you as well.
So why do we wait and pretend
As if this is not so.
Why would we not just close our
Eyes and extend each other soft
Kisses to help us both fly...

Love me as I love you right back.

Mak'in Love

Just think'in about the sweat roll'in down my chest,
Not wanting to stop just cause it felt so damn good!
Wishing you're not to numb and can still feel my
sword plunging deep into the soul of your wonder.
Years of this excitement, raging and commanding
Me to drop to my knees and lap up your cherry
Coke love. Roll'in over the top and under the thigh.
Throwing one leg behind my back, as my blackness
lifts you to screams of passion.

My Lord!

Sweet Sexy

Sweet sexy thing,
Let me bounce you around.
We can do this funky thing.
Let me toss it all around.

Let me dive into the
Back of you, spilling
Over, down your leg.

Feel so damn good,
Don't want to stop.
May act like you don't
Know how to behave.

Let's open our minds
And both feel fine and
Do this sweet sexy thing
All the time...

Sharing

*Sharing one's self with another one
Must be somewhat hard.
Looking at the big world along with
It's many parallels and dangers,
One could only wonder how
It could happen at all.
Opening doors from within,
Trusting one that is not the mother or kin.
Trusting enough to extend or receive
A kiss that could very well be contaminated.
So how do we come together?
How are we able to believe enough,
Without being foolish?
Is it the sight of the soul that allows us to
Freely express our true feelings from within
And even then and after, we can find
Ourselves to be so very wrong.
Well, I guess it's always worth a try,
Unless you really don't mind
Living your life alone.*

Say babe

What color is the sky for you today?
Is the blue as blue as can be?
Does the sun shine over you even in the dark?
Is your body warm from head to toe?
Full of love and peace,
Can you hear my words
Course through your veins as I write?
Does your sex drip from thinking
Of my kiss and hands
Running over your body?
Missing me as I miss you by candlelight.
To bathe in rose petals and wash each other
In soft oils so our bodies can meet
In a slide that last forever.
You and I and our families coming together as one,
Rejoicing over our love.
Happy we found each other and knowing
Our love is divine.
Oh, my love,
How I miss you much.
My body weeps from not being able
To look into your beautiful eyes now,
From not being able to reach out
And touch your hand or smell the
Florescent scent, that lifts to the heavens from you
Until this dark clock grants us the time
To be near each other again, I will die slowly.
With every second, comes a tear to run over my heart.
With every hour away, the numbness takes over my
body parts, making it impossible to move and
With everyday apart my heart breaks!
Come to me soon my princess

For the life is lifeless without you near.
Your love forever

Faith Alone

Is it true, I don't know you?
Can it be so, that we never meet before?
Never crossed paths on yesterday's streets.
Can it be?
Then why do I feel like we need not words?
How come I understand fresh flowers in your bath,
Makes you happy?
Why do I know the only kiss you will welcome, is
One of the softest truth.
How can I say if we never crossed paths before?
All the times we danced alone or with the wrong one,
Looking for each without knowing.
Knowing it's just around the corner but never
Coming quite enough.
How can I close my eyes and see every line and
curve that carve you.
The tears you carry because you can't change
The world.
Your questions of love and doubt, wondering if it just
exist in Hollywood movies of make believe.
How did I know to save myself,
Turning down all walks of life, abandoning my
Hopes of happily ever after, proud saying,
"If it takes a lifetime, I will wait forever".
How can it be, we've never meet and if so, why?
How could life make us wait so long?
So many winters passing with time.
Waiting for what's unseen. Living on faith alone.
Missing someone I've never meet.
Knowing you were out there somewhere.
Knowing one day, you would hear my voice
And we would be reunited.
How do I know this, if we never meet before?

Why is it so clear to me, seeing your eyes fold
As we make love with thunder till we both
Fall fast asleep in each other's arms.
Why can I see so clear and know you know
The same?
Whatever wonders freed us to be together,
Is one I pray will remain. For to lose you again,
Is to take breath from my lungs.
Leaving me without air, numb to the world to
Pick flowers for myself.
So if we never meet before,
Let me introduce myself forever.

Give Thanks

Rising 2 another morning.
Feeling the sun melt away the dew that has
Hardened through the night from dreams of you.
Feeling it drip down and over my body to see
You not.
Reaching out, heart and mind to just reminds
Of what was.
I truly miss you my love and wish you miss as well.
I invite you to come and celebrate life with me.
To rejoice and give thanks for the day.
In the sun as friends with no press from any other
than the cool breeze that may pass by your neck.
Share this day with me my love and let's give thanks.

Dinner

To be able to dine in your presence would
Awaken every morsel that may lie on my lips.
To be taken by time and forced to work,
May leave me limp and unfulfilled but,
To laugh at time and rest in your grace and
Dine till we say, "When",
Is the way one should enjoy their meal.
Till the sun goes and shares its might with
Others and falls to the backside of our world,
As we share grapes so sweet.
Till then and only then, can we think of a
more relaxing time in deed?

So dine,
I say dine!

Morning

You're so sweet as you sleep.
Watching you rolling awake with
A smile of pure truth and sunshine.
Oh, good morning to you love.
It's a beautiful day and it's waiting
For our goodness and joy.
They're singing outside our
Window songs from above,
Greeting us with welcome to the day.
She is yours and you're hers so
Embrace the day and know it's truth.

Tears

Tears
['tear] water drop;
1. emotional out pour;
uncontrollable feelings
joy, pain.

11

Own Tears

So then you close your eyes
And find yourself in the dark.
No windows,
No doors leading to any exits of any form.
No noise,
No air.
Just darkness.
Suddenly you hear a faint sound
Thump through this stillness of dark.
You know not where it comes
From as it grows louder.
You find yourself going mad with fear,
Hearing this thump grow louder and louder.
As you feel all reality close in,
You realize that your cheeks are wet
And the sound that was driving you crazy
In the dark was your own tears
Hitting the floor.

Love your Heart

I love your heart, is what she said.
I can see it pure. I can see you in my life
Forever together.
We will stop the wars, clearing
Away yesterday's bad news.
Always treating each other with love.
Never will you be used.
You can trust me and my love.
A tear I will never make you shed.
We can love as man should.
Never another in my bed.
I love your heart, is what she said,
Because of this I can always love you.
There will always be flowers blooming,
Even in the darkest room.
We both have been hurt so now I deem never more,
There will now only be love, love and then
Love more.
I love your heart, is what she said.
It refuels my life to fly.
It's too bad that all your words,
Were nothing but lies.
Still waiting for love.

Faith

I think I'm too sad to go on. I can read the signs.
I can see what's at the end of that road.
Been there before and no, it's no fun.
Strongman they say,
Better not cry, have no mercy.
Never thought it applied to the heart.
A safe place for those with one.
A bound amongst friends.
No rules but just plain fairness for the
Other heart beating in your arms.
Trial and error but, still that heart
Beating and throbbing for the other.
I guess no one's safe.
No one that decides to play the
Game of love has a chance to gain love.
Sounds like I'm not convinced anymore.
Sounds like a tear in the rain.
It's not and it is.
It's the yearning for food,
that delicatessen, that treat.
It's realization and growth
For hopes of better days.
It's tomorrow, got to breathe and face the signs again.
It's the questions and the doubts,
If we were even friends.
Happily ever after a fairytale I've believed.
Now I'll be happy with after because love,
It's just hard to believe.

Someplace

Promises

Oh, please help me Lord,
For I am dying.
The flowers are falling off
The vine and the wind chill
Is freezing my heart forever.
Oh, what life can do.
How we weep so behind
Shielded cages we call home
And what of love, that poison
That teases of happily ever after,
Only left to understand that
There is no happy ending.

It's over

Time seems so short when you love
And love is lost to the spoils of ourselves.
Watching the hand draw closer to the next hour.
The next click and goodbye to your dreams forever.
Who could be more wrong than two
That have proclaimed love to each other.
Two, that then could not find a way.
Better days do come but it could never
Be the same without each other.
"Turn your back with ease", you say,
"Forget", for it's not worth the fight anymore.
The tears are heavy and they flow more to see
That they mean nothing to anyone but the one
Spilling them out to the wind.
It's over...It's over...
The last petal on the flower that said, "Love me not".
The best is all we can wish for.
Glad we are smart enough to go.
Confident that it was not all that and
Better lies waiting around the corner.
Wishing the worst for things
We use to wish the best for.
Another women's scent and another man's strong
back to help us get over the time we wasted.
Maybe one will never look back?
Maybe one will never forget...
Maybe the angels are just laughing above
For Cupid has lost his arrow with a final
Shot to our ass, rather than to our hearts.
How can this be?
How can time and experience
Not make it clear what to expect?

*How can love fool and direct us to believe
in happily ever after when it's so clear that
It was just all made up for kids that
Did not know better.*

Don't give up

To hell with you, oh sweet love.
How dare you pry open the gates to my heart?
To hell with you for reminding
Me of the scent of a rose!
For shinning sunlight upon
My dream of love in the dark!
For letting me sleep upon thy
Breast and kiss your soft hand?
To hell with you for letting mine
Eyes fall upon you and you call me your man?
Lost forever after to only know your name.
Love me not to go away.
To curse my name for trying to
Love, love more,
You, in the rain.
To hell with you my love
For now I am alone and this pain
I cannot bear more.
Let me to my dark hole.
I do not want to know love again.
Not a flower,
To hold hands
Or midnight walks in the sand.
No new children to play at my feet,
Not even a butterfly I see,
For my heart is too weak.
To hell with you my love
These words I'll never speak,
Again.
To hell with you love,

What a stupid game.

The Dark

So what of tomorrow?
Will it really come?
If so, in what form?
Cold and wet or warm to the touch?
Will those sharing my air respect the land
Or will they stomp about in their big shoes,
Killing my bed of flowers forever.
So what?
Love a wish granted in truth.
Will she find me in the dark
And if so, will she have strength
Enough to still see that love is here?
I fear she will walk past and only see
A shadow of what she wanted as well and
Who can blame her.
The life can blind the purest of hearts.
I pray she sees me over all the life to come,
Otherwise I fear I too will be lost forever in the dark...

Matters not

I know not what to think of this tragedy or
If you can even understand how you hurt me so?
I guess it matters not for to each, his own.
I hope that God will take you out of my heart
And mind soon for everyday that passes,
I grow angrier and harder only because I thought
I had a good plan for forever but,
Now I see that love is only in the individuals heart.
You can offer it, scream it from a mountaintop
Or long and cry all day for it but it matters not
If the one you love can't hear you.

Please God don't harden me so
And take this hate away from my soul.

Hearing Heals

Waking in the middle of the night
Reaching out to yesterday.
Still hearing heals coming down the hall,
Attached to candy apple lingerie and ruby red lips.
Still can hear the laugh so loud from the thrill
Of fast boats and planes that fly.
Waking in the middle of the night,
Reaching out to yesterday's lie.
Still missing all of her little ways.
Little nick knacks and pottery from foreign lands.
The baths by candle light and how long
They would last.
Still remembering black curls lying down
Her back, wondering forever after.
Where could she be?
If she walks in the night as well.
If she cries and burns, like she's in hell.
If she thinks of me.
Spoke to her the other day and she said
She still loves me.
She even sounded like she would cry you see.
Still waking to the sound of heals coming
Down the hall.
Opening my eyes to see it's dark.
It was a dream,
That's all.
Still waking to yesterday's dreams,
Only able to remember.

Just Falling

Sick and sad to see myself today.
Holding back, saying to myself,
Thinking there's a falling angel for me out there.
Finding most just falling and praying for myself
And others. Unable to practice what I preach for
I have found none that has heard my message
Besides those that could only share a friendship
Along side of me. For I have extended a kiss to one
but in the later I have found that the sweet kiss
I extended was only taken out of curiosity.
Used as a blanket to cover all the madness in
Their world for that short time.
Nothing real about it.
Explaining that all was put on the table from
The start and no feelings were to be included
In that union we had.
And I the fool, accepting it, not wanting to believe
the words spoken.
Only looking at heart and believing it
Could not be so and the love would shine
Over all, allowing us to have Happily Ever After.
Then I woke up and heard the screams in the
Streets and the madness around.
I was left where I was standing without even a friend.
Made to understand that this was no fallen angel.
Just one that wanted another life for a second
And decided I could be the one to release her from
Her yesterday. So she was released and in the end she
flew away with some of my goods and called me
friend as she went on to the next.

I hope that all is more than well around you and your warm in your soul.

Love lost

So now the tears start to flow.
See I'm on my way to somewhere else
And I know not what I do.
Left love because love left me.
Then why do I cry and hurt so?
How can I be clear with a heart so clouded?
And what of the untold tomorrow?
Will mercy be shown to hearts filled red?
Will anyone care if I die a horrible death?
And will love ever rest from haunting my life?
Tonight I'll cry myself to sleep just because
It seems like love has been forgotten by time
And I, I am left to live without,
Love...

Never Over

Open your eyes to the
Shadows that block out the sun.
Open your mind to the jesters
From those around.
There is a way through the maze
That lies at your feet.
There is a way around your
Dreams and beliefs.
You can't change something that is.
You can't accept or reject something that is.
It is not your choice.
You have no control.
You think if you get A's on your report card,
Mommy won't hit you anymore.
You think if you give all then you're finished,
You won't be hurt anymore.
You think they will understand.
Don't be surprised.
How could you not?
Don't be angry because you're surprised.
Don't be stupid!
No matter how one looks at it,
The river must flow.
To try and block it and bear the pressure building,
Is a stronger man than I?
I can't sum up the pain.
I can't cry any louder than I have.
I must live, as I know how.
I have to remember me and go forward.
I must not ignore the lessons I've learned
And I must always remember the signs.
I guess the pain in a way is good for

*In the end it does make you remember
who you are and where you came from.*

Most Don't Care

Hard to walk through all this stuff man has laid
Out over the road.
Speechless looking around, discovering that
Most don't care or are too blind to see the damage
They left behind.
I can't understand it.
I can't believe you are so lost and harder to
Think that you will ever be found.
Stern fist beating hard against the concrete.
Beating till hands are full of nothing but blood,
For you have nothing better to do
And know not your way home.
Shame on you for losing sight of yourself
And ill-treating your brother.
There is not much left of your reminds
For there is little that is good I see.
In your world you may have won at your game
But in mine you are forever a fool.

Where do we go

Where have we went to?
What happened to all the dreams?
How could hate and rage run over
The same heart that bled for love?
Can it be that our efforts have been in vain?
Can it be that I have failed at love again?
What will it take for me to understand?
Where must I go to find it?
Is it just that I'm cursed to roam?
Should I just be happy I have children
To hang with till I'm gone?
I just am upset because it's what
I've wanted and it's what I tried. I tried for
from my heart and gave just the same.
Maybe I've exposed too much of myself,
Thinking it was o.k.?
Maybe I asked too much for you to give?
Maybe I should have overlooked it all?
I don't know.
I've loved and tried and never thought my
Works would become nothing more than this.
I will live with my faults and be what you
Think in your mind knowing in reality
The truth could never be a lie.

Got to fly

Goodbye my friend,
Guess I got to go.
Never thought it could hurt so much,
When I had to say so.

I'm crying and hurting
Because yes you, I adore.
Knowing I turned my back
Very possibly can mean, No more!

No more late night movies,
Missed because we were late.
No more sugar soft kisses,
Excited every time like a first date.

The things we do for love
Can only kill us and leave us for dead.
Lots of hoping and crying,
Never knowing where,
where we are lead.

So we have to be strong,
Walk my friend with pride.
Just remember love, love more
And from it, try not to hide.

The death will be slow
And painful without a sign.
All from trying to love,
Only wishing forever mine.

Sometimes

Sometimes it's just hard to breathe
Even if there is enough air for all.
Sometimes it's very dark even
If the sun is shinning bright.
Sometimes it's very cold
Even if the hearts of the children
Playing around are warm.
Sometimes you just have to believe.

Planet

['planet] n a large body in space that moves around a star. A nonluminous celestial body, illuminated by light from stars.

12

Who Are You

Who are you and what are you made of?
Can you hear when a child cries in the other room?
Do you feel when there are some going hungry
in other parts of our world?
Are the old just dust, blown in the wind
in your mind?
Is the dollar spending you instead of you spending it?
And who will stand and change our world?
Who will stand and change our world?
Who will make a difference and is there any possibility
that that person could be you?

Dirty Streets

Dirty streets, filth from man, won't they learn.
How can we bear more?
Must we all burn.
Was the heavens right to flood the land to
Wash away all the dirt we have made.
Looking at our world many years later,
Clearly sending me to my grave.
My heart aches.
I cry and fear for all of us around.
I fear for our child,
For tomorrow looks unsound.
Seems like the basic laws of the land may be lost.
Now there's only concrete jungles
Made of cash to separate all of us.
The ones that have not, have long given up hope.
In their eyes one can see death,
Tomorrows already blown up.
For those that have,
Their smiles are impossible to find.
To get where they are,
It seems they left their dreams behind.
If people still care,
It is truly hard to see.
Even in different parts of our world,
There's still slavery.
I fear even a flood can't clean the streets I see.
I can't even see how people can even be happy.
Tears in my eyes for the children that must still grow,
Maybe there's hope in them,
Maybe, at least in one,
Who knows?
I myself will forever stand tall.

I will try to do, as I should.
To be a good man, good man and be good.

Maybe some ways will rub off.
Maybe it will even help one.
Maybe in the end the smallest change
Can help some children see the sun.
If I had one last prayer,
I will pray for cleaner streets.
I will pray we as man,
Learn a better way to see.

Amen

Harvest

So, choices to make again.
Questions within unknown tomorrows.
Wishing only for the best 4 the child.
Drawbacks and doors leading to nowhere.
The leap of life falling aimlessly at your
Feet leaving with the mandatory action,
To take it and deal.
Fighting man's normal actions while forgiving
the ones that may wish you harm.
So why shouldn't I beg for mercy?
How could I not shed painful tears?
After toiling the soil for so long
We naturally expect the grass to grow.
A flower to bloom in any color,
It is our reward for that long life's work.
As the seasons change from hot to cold and
Winds change directions, we look toward the
Garden we have tended for and when we may
celebrate and partake of her harvest.

Home

Nice to hear laughter in the streets from
Those that simply share the day with me.
Joy from within,
Out bursting into loud sounds that echo
Like shots in a hall just because no one
Else around can say a word.
I think now, looking toward journeying
Back to my own homeland that I missed,
That simple laughter crying out in one
Way or another.
Regardless of cash or social status,
There has always been enough
Strength to laugh and not just for I,
But for all my kind that have suffered
And withstood more or less the same.
So now I have to laugh myself at the
Little things we miss and see
When we're away from home.

More

Well, what did you really expect?
Knew exactly what would follow because
Man is forever comical.
Forever able to show their fangs before they push
them deep in your neck and take your blood.
So caught up in social madness, walking around,
Not even able to see thy own stupid face
In the mirror.
Following a fool's path made by foolish man.
Even the bible is turned into Amazon dot com
And ripped apart without reason.
And who has a problem with the
Ten Commandments anyway?
Man so stupid.
So wrong and naive.
I pray for something other than
Another great flood to clean our streets.
In the meantime I think it would be best
To keep my way and lead another path for
My child to follow.
More sunshine,
More rainbows,
More sea sounds,
More butterfly kisses,
More love,
More emotion,
More faith,
More children
And more heart.

Funny

So funny at times,
The man building his world brick by brick.
So eager to make the world bigger than it already is.
Planning tomorrow through T.V
And real life fairy tales come true.
Rules ruled by man.
Rules made by man.
Rules broken by man.
It's like setting traps for one's own foot.
If man is to make these rules for man,
Then one could only think they would
Follow them rather than find themselves
Trapped within them.

Is it so

Is it so and are we so messed upon
This planet we call our home?
So hard to believe at times.
Astonishing and scary.
Bend love and give it a new name.
No one's looking and if they were,
They probably won't even care.
Sickness multiplied and passed on
From generation to generation,
Then broadened and explained
To children that wonder why
They are so messed up as well.

Let's tell the truth just once.
Let's be truthful with ourselves at least
And act like we were under our Grandmas care,
With a little more respect than we pretend
Is acceptable.

There is still time.

Be Counted

Taking your place in the ranks.
Looking through eyes of blood red full.
Unable to trust even the air you breathe
From fear of contamination of some sort.
Friends called friends because they know
Your name and families excusing their cruel
Words because they are brother.
Walking as ghost around those near just
Because they can't really see you.
Forever wishing for just another
Day of sunshine to warm our spirits.
Caught atop a mountaintop naked and alone.
Feeling the ifs running through your mind.
Leaving you paralyzed with fear from the feet up.
Sword drawn in the ready stands for
Whatever comes in through the door.
Regrets are none in this game, for everyone is
playing for keeps. If none have to be speared,
They won't, for we need no witnesses to tell the tell.
All that's needed to be known is that
More awaits you in your tomorrow,
If for the better or the worst, balance upon
A moving planet that forever is growing.
We are truly just guest upon it and I am sad
To say, not great ones.
I fear that sooner or later if we do not change
directions our invitations will be revoked and
We all kicked off to another place.
This much is clearer than all the sands blown
About at one time.
Clean and ready yourself for you all will be counted.

Our air

The wind blowing about.
Sometimes warm full of the sun.
Sometimes bitter, crisp and cold as can be.
Blowing around the world.
Being shared by all that breathe.
One love, one air for all walks of man.
One can wonder if this wind actually blows
Completely around the world at one point,
Returning to the same place it blew from the start?
To think in this manner, one must realize that
We all needed and shared its one sweet scent.
I can see how us as human can be blown about
In like fashion at times.
Our directs moved by instinct to move but,
Without knowing, finding ourselves in the same
Place we began at one point or another.
Can you hear the flute's music being pushed by air,
Producing such a sound we call music.
Blown by man, with air from man, that was shared
By other man at one time or another.
The air in the wind or the wind in the air,
Ending in the out of a flute that we as man call music.

Ever so clear

Surrounded by non-believers.
Those that have lost their way shortly after birth.
A whole nation that thinks of themselves less
Than unique.
Caught up in dreams of make up,
Makes you look better or new tennis
Shoes make you jump higher.
Over drunk and high.
Children that only can say,
"Forget you mom! No Dad".
Trying to be their own person but backing
Up this need with hard disrespectful actions
That only deems respect if you're caged like an
Animal in a cell being shoved food over a course
Of assembly lines that you may die in before you
even get served.
Hopeless it seems on the surface.
Impossible for any type of light to shine through
This thick cloud of confusion.
And why shouldn't one cry just from the day?
How could things so easily be this way?
If my memory serves me correctly,
There are great elders with lessons to spare.
Lessons not handed down in book form but ones
spilled thick over time in the form of blood and
The loss of children that only know how to play.
Did everyone stop listening?
Has the elders all died off or have they just grown
Tired of pushing air to their lips to speak and not
Be heard, not be understood, not a one to give
A damn. I can see in my own keen eyes the fatigue
and hope lost from the thought that none will survive

this story and we all may end up dead, leaving our child to be tended for by others that know how to teach something other than great.
And some wonder why I have left this mad Land years ago. Funny for my eyes are ever so Clear and I see the truth in this sad song and it Pushes tears to my eyes for there definitely Should be better after all this time and pain from Too many a mother. At a time we believed the child would grow and sooth the pains of their parents, That they would help bring them above the level They already reached. Instead, the children are coming In and taking the last drop of Kool-Aid and leaving the mothers of the world more wicked than they were before they bore life to them.
Who is the messenger?
The dove to find the fig leaf of life and deliver us. Who is that human soul with the voice to be heard and the will to endure.
Could it be me, you and if so, will the life we live in today give us a chance to tell the story.

I Can

I can't hear you people
And you have so much to say,
Words used in another way.
Sharing with thy brother man,
Adding a different color
To those that may hear.
What a gift to give,
And a gift to receive.
Words, words
And more words,
From me 2 you I share.

Closed doors

If it be so, let my stomach turn, for I not agree.
Desire, hidden in the closet, behind closed doors.
Regardless of today's trouble, tomorrow's rainbows
Shine bright.
I am no object, no matter, no man.
I lead not the path laid by man and I will not imitate
Their heartless behavior.
Lord please lead my steps.
Love, love more seems so far away.
Knowing I only wish harmony within my walls,
Peace around the world and a love as one.
As for man's comical ways of drama beyond
T.V and war.
I pray daily while I pray for better ways.
Life is truly life, what a wonderful word.
May we all partake in her fruits and bathe in her
Sister sun.
Togetherness globally, friends in family and love
towards thy mate.
Love, love more,
you can understand.

Planet Round

Looking around at golden bridges,
Pointed tower and water holes made of granite.
Open seas leading to far off lands
And curious imaginations.
Looking upon my home and seeing clear
The possibilities that are forced in our face.
Seeing that days are numbered and there
Are those out there that can only find joy in
Bringing it all down.
Flashing to Independence Day and seeing
How Hollywood has made well in showing
Us our own destruction without mercy.
Looking ever so around and wondering
If my eyes will look upon these same years
From now and if my children's children
Will be so blessed.
Will we be able to survive all this?
Man is catching up with themselves and tearing
Down the buildings that they built.
Killing all the flowers and thinking they are doing so,
for some good, some religion, some God.
Teaching the young hate as they proclaim
righteousness in it because they are older
And are suppose to know from the ill lessons
Taught in the past.
We are scary.
Worst than any monster movie and a
Thousand times sicker.
Looking round, you can see that we are dead wrong
and none can really be proud of themselves for
the small steps taken.
We are truly sinners and I know not

If this time we will be forgiven.
Our acts must be for the better.
We are responsible for all this noise
And need to correct the wrongs we made,
If we are to be whole and live longer.
Family's Friends Lovers all must change together,
At one time to turn this planet round the other way.
It is our only hope.

Senseless Murder

*So my eyes are clear and Senseless Murder
Leads the way. Leading us to self-destruction
By our own hand. There is a war ahead that will
Leave us all without sleep.
Almost too late for there are only a few that are
chosen to lead us out of this dark ahead.
All lead by love of the purest clutched tight
Within hearts. Will unbreakable by hate
Or the same.
New Saviors, New Messiahs to lead the way
And show us those colors needed seen to brighten
Our hearts and open doors that are of much
Clearer paths.
Now I cry out at the top of my lungs as I vow
My commitment to the role I openly accept.
All of I, I give to change the Senseless Murder
Running amuck in our streets around the world.
My tear's shell now run as blood rather than of
The pretty blues I once remembered.
The solider to battle till death to spread
Love and peace around our world.
I pray for strength to bear what my eyes may see
Tomorrow and ask for forgiveness of mine own sins.
Our children must be allowed to grow.
Our children must be allowed to grow!
They must be given a chance outside of the
Dirty wind that we man have made and they will!*

www.ingramcontent.com/pod-product-compliance
Lightning Source LLC
Chambersburg PA
CBHW031240290426
44109CB00012B/380